A Cat Named Squeeky

ISBN: 978-0-9800235-0-3

Author's Note

All the described events involving Squeeky in this story are true.

For reasons of personal privacy, some names of characters appearing in this story have been changed. Some haven't. It's nothing serious. I figured those who exhibited questionable behavior would prefer to remain anonymous. I sure would.

In a few instances, minor supporting events or dialogue, although based on reality, were recreated in a dramatic fashion for literary purposes (made up), to keep the story fun and interesting. This also serves to hide the fact that my memory is not what it used to be.

But the important stuff is all true.

Really.

Those are the things I'll never forget.

Dedication

To all pets who've come and gone
and to their owners who miss them.

This one's for you.

Contents

A Cat Named Squeeky

Raining Cats And Dogs

It had been a rainy December day in our small town of Los Gatos, California.

The big Eucalyptus tree in the back yard was throwing its bark off in the howling wind like a snake shedding its skin. Three and four foot lengths of bark littered the patio in back and the driveway alongside our house.

Standing inside and looking out the back window, I watched a large black cloud hang over the mountains east of town and listened to the rain hitting the roof overhead.

It was a steady drumbeat of rain.

"Rat-a-tat-tat, rat-a-tat-tat, rat-a-tat-tat . . ."

The rain was coming down "in buckets" as some might say.

Others might have described the weather as "raining cats and dogs."

In fact, that was the very phrase my wife, Cindy, used as she ran out of the house to go shopping. As she ran across the front lawn toward our car parked in the driveway she said, "It's raining cats and dogs."

I watched the rain come down and I began to think about the phrase "raining cats and dogs." I thought it rather bizarre. I mean, if you think about it, it really makes no sense at all.

If somebody says it's raining cats and dogs, the picture I get in my mind is of a bunch of furry bodies hurtling toward the earth from out of the sky. Like an invasion of alien animals from the planet Chihuahua.

I see clumps of sopping wet poodles hanging in the trees, beagles rolling around in mud puddles and howling at absolutely nothing, and lots of cats and dogs everywhere: striped ones, black ones, fat ones. Cats and dogs of all colors and sizes. I see a pretty good rainfall and everything else is a mess of legs and tails swinging off of bodies heavy with rain-drenched fur and the soggy fur is hanging down in clumps of thick, water-soaked strands.

Now THAT'S raining cats and dogs!

That would be the kind of rain no cat or dog would want to find itself in. When it's "raining cats and dogs" do you ever see a cat or dog outside in the rain?

No way.

Not unless it had to be there through no conscious decision or fault of its own, a cruel victim of life imitating art. The artwork entitled:

<u>Placed in the Watery Woods</u>
<u>by Fate's Own Hand</u>
<u>without a Bone to Beg for</u>
<u>or a Voice calling it Home.</u>

Meteor Museum. $10 Admission

As it got darker and wetter outside, I decided that I hated the rain.

It's good for farmers and umbrella designers. They've got a personal financial stake in the matter. Sure. I'd be for volcanoes and spider attacks if I could make a buck off either one.

Fishermen like the rain if there's enough of it to create rivers and lakes.

Various species of aquatic life also enjoy the benefits of rain if they can avoid the fishermen.

Then there are squirt-gun manufacturers, plumbers, kids in summer with inner tubes heading for a lake, kids in winter with ice skates heading for the same lake. Oh, there's a list as long as your left arm that makes up this self-centered lot who could care less if you have to walk in the rain with a bag of groceries, whose wet bottom is about to give way and your neck is getting wet and your feet are getting cold and your house is three blocks away.

I hate driving in the rain because I often can't see a darn thing, including other drivers who, if I can't see them, probably can't see me not seeing them, and one of these days two "can't sees" is going to add up to one big "Uh oh!"

I hate hearing the rain on the roof because it reminds me of an awful seven year period when the roof leaked without any concern for those down below. I couldn't afford to hire someone to repair the roof, and I wasn't able to patch the leaks myself because I couldn't find the rain's entrance points. At times I could almost feel the rain taking pleasure in coming through the roof and ceiling and dribbling onto the living room floor, as if it were a mystical force able to pass through a solid object and then reappear on the other side.

3

"Don't get cocky," I'd yell at the rain. "You ain't no David Copperfield. It's not you that's special. It's the roof that's shitty!"

The best I was able to do was place sheets of thick plastic in various spots in the attic to catch the water before it hit the ceiling. During any sizable rainstorm several little pools of water would form on top of the plastic sheets. One time the leaks were in pretty much the same area, so one large pool of water formed up in the attic. It looked like a little kid's wading pool. I would've invited some neighborhood kids to come over and go sloshing around in my attic except I was afraid the whole mess might come crashing down into the house.

I hoped that someday a meteor, careening to earth, would slam into my roof, and vaporize all those aging, rotting roof parts and miraculously leave the rest of the house intact.

I would turn the house into a meteor museum and charge admission for folks to come up in the attic and see what an actual meteor could do. They could touch some of the meteor parts lying around. I'd have some tiny bottles containing meteor dust for sale, on a key chain. Kids would love it. They could give one to their dads on Father's Day.

But, of course, none of this ever happened. I eventually had to hire a roofer to replace the roof. It cost me $4,000. Now you know why I am not fond of the rain.

On this particular night, it was a tossup as to who disliked the rain more, me, or the cat that was looking at me through a window pane in the back door.

Looking Out, Looking In

From the inside, our back door usually looks like this.

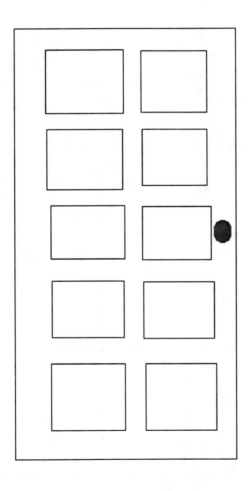

That night it looked like this .

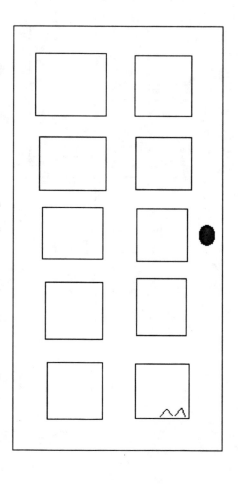

Coffee Can Cat

I told Cindy, who was in the kitchen, that there was somebody at the back door and that she should go see who it was.

"Who would come to the back door?" she said.

"Just go see."

"Why wouldn't the person go to the front door?" she said.

"Hurry up," I said.

"There's nobody there, is there?" she said. She thought I was making wise.

"Hurry," I said.

"Why should I hurry if there's nobody there?"

"You're going to miss it."

"Miss what?"

Cindy was not going to take the bait. She was not going to let me surprise her with the cat at the back door. Which of itself was an unusual occurrence. We had lived in our house for six years and not once during that time had a cat stuck its face up to the back door.

Once we had a raccoon in our neighbor's oak tree.

It was a big raccoon with a big butt. He didn't stay in the tree very long.

Then there was the time an owl roosted in the Eucalyptus tree for a few days. He looked tough and weathered, his feathers sticking out all over the place like he'd been in a wrestling match with something a bit bigger than himself.

A few possums would show up in the summertime and root around in the bushes alongside the house. Their nighttime snorting and snuffling woke me up several times.

That was the extent of the animal life we had experienced in our yard until this cat showed up.

I went to the back door to let the cat in. I wanted to see if it had an identification tag. If it belonged to one of the neighbors around us, I'd let it make its own way home. But if it came from somewhere farther up the street, or maybe from another part of town, I thought I'd drive it home, with the weather being nasty and all.

As I approached the back door, the cat looked up at me with its eyes big and round, then quickly turned around and scooted down the back steps.

I opened the door and looked down at our patio trying to see the cat, but I couldn't spot it. It was getting dark outside, too dark to distinguish a flower pot from a large rock, or a cat from the empty coffee can that was lying on its side under our patio table.

Too bad that cat couldn't find a way to squeeze into that coffee can and stay there until the storm passed, I thought. A coffee can shelter was better than no shelter at all.

"So what'd I miss?" Cindy said, coming to the back door.

"A cat," I said.

"Really?"

"Really."

"Right at the back door?"

"Yep."

"Was it one of the neighbor's cats?"

"I don't think so. I didn't get a real good look at it. But I didn't recognize it."

"Maybe somebody on our street got a new cat and it's checking out the neighborhood."

"Could be." I said.

"Or maybe it's lost."

"Also a possibility," I said.

"Should we try to find it?" Cindy said as she looked out the back window, down at the patio, trying to spot the cat.

"It took off pretty fast," I said. "It's probably gone. Besides, it's getting dark. I doubt if it's still around."

But Cindy continued to look outside. She had a worried look on her face.

"I'll go take a quick look around the house," I said.

8

I put on a coat and walked down the back steps. It wasn't raining at the moment. I looked around the patio and didn't see the cat. I walked up the driveway to the front of the house and looked around the front yard. No cat. I figured the heck with it. After all, it wasn't my cat out on a night like this.

I went back down the driveway and started to go up the back steps to go inside. I looked over at the table which was in the middle of the patio, then I walked over to it and reached underneath it and picked up the coffee can. I put the coffee can in the garbage. The wind was getting stronger and an empty coffee can could have rolled around that patio all night.

Like A Crow With A Sore Throat

By the next morning the storm had passed.

Huge white clouds hung motionless against a brilliant blue background, like soldiers in the sky patiently waiting for field commands from an unseen commander.

Then the commander, wearing a big hat, says in a big voice:

"Steady now, clouds. I said STEADY CLOUDS! I see movement over the Santa Cruz Mountains. Will the group over downtown San Jose stop billowing immediately? All cumulo-nimbus be prepared to scud in a northerly direction as the high pressure weakens. When air currents hit twenty knots I expect the horsetail group to resume an attractive feathery display."

While the clouds hovered in their pool of blue, I decided to clean the back yard of the storm's debris. All around me were oak and eucalyptus leaves, twigs, big chunks of eucalyptus bark, and bits and pieces of branches from our neighbor's Bay tree.

I was raking all this stuff into one big pile, which I would smash and cram into our garbage can whose weight would probably cause our garbage man to consider another line of work, when I heard something that startled me.

It came from behind me.

Which is why it startled me.

I don't like noises from behind me.

And this wasn't really what you would call a noise.

It was more like . . . a sound.

A strange sound which I couldn't quite place.

It sounded . . . sort of like . . . a sound that a crow with a swollen sore throat might make.

But it wasn't a "caw" or a "screech" or a "squawk."

10

It was not two tree branches rubbing against each other in a breeze. It wasn't a slowly opening wooden door, which would have been identifiable as a "creak." The sound was part tight cork being removed from a wine bottle, part rubber-soled basketball shoe pivoting on a hardwood floor, and part 1967 Ford pickup door swinging on a rusted hinge.

I also judged that the source of the sound was not from a vegetable or mineral source. Which could only mean that it came from . . . an ANIMAL!

As I slowly turned to check out what type of beast was coming up on my backside, and wondered if it was smooth-skinned or long-tailed and did it have sharp teeth, it made its distinctive sound once again.

It's difficult to find the exact word in the English language that evokes this sound, the blended mix of twisting cork and sliding shoe and swinging door, but there is one word that comes as close as any to duplicating what I heard behind me.

That word is "eek."

Veggie Burger Anyone?

I turned around not quite sure what to expect.

We had alligator lizards on the property. I try to be kind to all animals, including the slithery ones, but I really don't care for the alligator lizards. They give me the creeps. They look like shrunken relatives of a much larger species from a prehistoric era, and I know if they got half a chance to put on a few pounds, they'd try to take back the planet they once dominated.

I stay out of their way. Sharon Stone's husband didn't and he got his foot bit by a large Komodo lizard.

I wondered if lizards had verbal abilities. Could they go "eek?"

In milli-micro seconds my brain flashed on the big-butted raccoon. Could he have come back? I know raccoons make some kind of chittering or clicking noises at night when they're rummaging around. But what other sounds could they make?

Ready to kick and fight, or if things looked dicey, bolt and run, I prepared myself mentally to confront the thing behind me. I turned to face the invader.

When I saw the creature I was relieved.

I could handle it.

It was no big deal.

It was a cat.

Not a big cat. It didn't look to be an old cat. But a very pretty multi-colored, slightly bigger than a breadbox cat that looked up at me with powder blue eyes and went "eek."

"Well, hello there," I said.

"Mareek," the cat answered. A different response. Two syllables with another sound preceding the "eek."

"Do you always creep up on people?" I said.

"Irrim," the cat said, now making a sound that resembled a cross between a hum and a growl.

"You could scare a person creeping up behind them like that, you know?" I said.

"Werp?" the cat said.

After every statement I made, the cat made a different verbal comment. It seemed I was having a conversation with a cat.

"Were you looking in my back door last night?" I said.

"Ee-eek," the cat said, now in two syllables again, as it looked intently into my eyes, unblinking, not looking away even for a split second.

I couldn't really tell if it was the same cat that I saw at my door the previous night. In the darkness, all I saw was the top of a cat's head and two pointy ears. It could have been the same cat. Probably was. It's not like there's a highway of cats going through our back yard.

"Hey, cat. Let me ask you something," I said. "Do you always say something when spoken to?"

Now the cat didn't say anything.

I stood with my arms crossed and looked down at the cat.

The cat sat on its haunches and looked up at me. A momentary lull in our conversation gave me the opportunity to look at the cat more closely.

It didn't have a collar or any kind of identifying name tag, but it didn't look scraggly or unkempt. Its coloring and markings were beautiful. It was a Siamese mix. Dark around the face, legs, and tail, and it had a swirl of tans and browns with white patches all over the rest of its body. Its chest and stomach area were completely white. The face looked like it was dipped in a hot fudge sundae, with a cream colored streak coming down the middle of its forehead and over its nose. The right side was more mottled and speckled than the left. It looked like the start of a Jackson Pollock painting of a cat. Then Jackson lost interest and swiped the left side of the cat's face with a broad stroke of brown, just before he left the studio saying, "That's enough for today" and then forgot to finish the painting.

The cat's eyes were a soft and powdery blue.

"Come here," I said, in a voice as soothing as I could manage. I didn't want to scare it. I thought I'd pet it a little and then let it go on its way.

13

I crouched down on my heels and slowly extended my right arm palm upward. It seems that somewhere I read or heard that when greeting an animal for the first time, you should slowly extend your arm with your palm turned upward, which is the way food is given to an animal (a good thing). If the animal sees your arm coming palm downward, it might perceive the gesture as a threatening or intimidating motion (a bad thing). The animal may choose to run away (an unfortunate thing). Or it may choose to bite you (a painful thing).

The cat didn't flinch. It sniffed my open palm and went "eek."

It looked a little on the skinny side and I thought it could use a snack. Then I thought, wait a second, this is probably somebody's cat. Maybe they wouldn't appreciate me feeding their cat. Maybe it was on a special diet. With all the health food freaks in Los Gatos, for all I knew this cat was raised on veggie burgers and some strange mush made from soybeans.

I stood up and looked down at the cat.

It walked in a tight semi-circle, flopped down on the ground, looked up at me, and said "eek" again.

I said "Right. Stay here and I'll go get you something to eat."

I went back inside the house to look for a bit of food that might interest a cat. I found cereal, bread, bagels, half a head of lettuce, some rubbery carrots, and a leftover tamale dish that we were going to have for dinner. Did cats like tamales? I considered it a possibility. They could like tamales as much as they like fish, and they have no business liking fish. I mean, why do cats like to eat fish so much?

I had never owned a cat, but I've had plenty of friends and relatives who've had a cat or two lurking around the house, and these cats all loved to eat fish, especially tuna. Their houses always smelled a touch strong.

I don't believe cats are considered an aquatic species. I don't recall seeing pictures of groups of cats swimming together in lakes, or jumping alongside salmon in the rivers of the Northwest, occasionally taking a bite out of a passing Chinook. Cats aren't found floating and bobbing in the waters of Monterey Bay off the California coast, masquerading as otters or very tiny seals, in preparation for their daily food run among schools of sardines.

So I'm thinking. Cats don't grow up a beaver's best buddy, yet they still love tuna. Maybe cats, or at least this one, might like tamales. I

14

knew this cat was part Siamese from its coloring. Maybe the other part was Mexican. Who could tell?

I put a little portion of the tamale on a plate and took it outside.

I looked for the cat but it was gone. I didn't see it anywhere.

It just took off.

Maybe it smelled the tamale coming.

Several Days Later

Several days later the weekend had arrived. I was repainting the handrails on the back steps when I heard a familiar sound off in the distance.

I looked across our patio into our neighbor's back yard and saw the cat with the hot fudge sundae face walking toward me. It didn't look right or left or stop to sniff at the most recent gopher hole at the edge of our patio. It just walked purposefully in my direction, yammering nonstop.

It kind if went "reek-reekrow-maw-meek" in a Morse Code of cat language. It was an interesting series of mutterings without a meow among them.

At that moment Cindy came out the back door and saw the cat. "Oh, what a pretty cat," she said. "Where'd he come from?"

"I don't know," I said. "He was hanging around a couple of days ago. Must be new in the neighborhood."

"Do you think he was the one at our back door the other night?" Cindy said.

"I'm not sure," I said. "It could have been."

"I don't see a collar on him," Cindy said. "Maybe he's a stray."

I picked the cat up in my arms. As I lifted it, it went "wee-urk." Yet another sound in its repertoire.

Cindy petted the cat's head and examined it closely.

"Allow me to make a minor correction," Cindy said. "I don't see a collar on her. This is a young lady who's visiting us."

The cat's body size was slightly smaller than your typical tabby cat, and she was young. She couldn't have been more than a year or two old.

She didn't have a collar on her, but that didn't mean the cat didn't belong to someone, who may have thoughtlessly never given her a collar

16

with an identification tag. How stupid! No name tag, no phone number, no address! How could a stranger, upon meeting a wandering pet, identify and greet an animal by its proper name without a way to identify it? "And how are you today, let's see, what does it say on your collar. . . Millicent. How are you today, Millicent?" Should the animal look confused and lost, its furry eyebrows v-shaped with worry, you could look at the address on its collar and say "Don't worry, Sugar Pop, I'm going to take you back to 236 University Ave. where you belong." Or if the animal was hunched up in a corner of your yard and unhealthily shaking with a case of the wooly vapors, you could place a phone call to the number on its shiny identification tag with the urgent message to "come get Morgan 'cause he's not looking too perky."

"Don't you think we should try and find out if she belongs to somebody in the neighborhood?" Cindy said. "Maybe she's lost or maybe she's run away."

"I suppose we should," I said looking down at the cat as it took a few steps toward me and then backed off, then walked in a circle and wound up rubbing up against Cindy's legs.

"Tell you what," I said. "Why don't I take her up and down the street, show her to the neighbors, and see if she belongs to anyone in the neighborhood."

"OK. Good luck," Cindy said.

I picked up the cat and hoisted her up on my left side, so she could place her front legs on top of my shoulder. Rather than cradling her in my arms, the shoulder position was a little bit easier for me to carry her some distance.

Then I wondered if it would bother her that she would be looking backwards as we went house-to-house, up and down our street. Would the forward motion in a backwards position physically upset a cat in some way? Make her dizzy? Upset her stomach? Make her upchuck? I didn't think that was likely to happen, then again, what did I know about cat behavior? Nothing. From the rearmost portion of my brain, where I placed the majority of my mother's cautionary warnings, came a nagging bit of advice, in my mother's voice. "Don't be stoooo-pid," the voice said. I put the cat down and went inside to change into a ratty sweatshirt. Just in case.

"Don't let her run away," I said to Cindy. "I'll be right back."

When I came back, Cindy was sitting on the back steps and watching the cat which was lying on its left side, then it flipped onto its right side, then it squirmed back the other way and stopped in mid-flip so that all four feet were in the air. With every motion the cat said something. I heard an "eek" and an "irk," even a "haarmpf."

I picked the cat up, and again, boosted her up on my shoulder. She went "waaark?"

"Let's go find out who you belong to," I said, walking down our driveway, carrying the cat like I did it all the time, like I delivered cats for a living.

The Neighbors

It was a certainty the cat didn't belong to the neighbors immediately to the right of us. They were big time bird lovers with a large bird feeder right in the middle of their back yard. Glen and Muriel are kind-hearted people and maintain a huge pile of bird seed in their bird feeder, which in actuality had once been a bird bath. Los Gatos creek ran nearby and I guess they figured the birds needed food more than they needed water.

All winged creatures who feasted at Glen and Muriel's bird feeder also enjoyed the protection of Muriel and her broom. Whenever Muriel saw a cat, she'd come running out of her house swinging that broom with two hands like it was a baseball bat. Any cat seeing Muriel in bird-defense mode immediately sprinted for its life. Cats know they are not meant to be home run balls, and there was no way that the cat peering over my left shoulder belonged to Glen and Muriel.

*   *   *

Next came the Dolans.

They were cat fanciers and had two black cats of their own. They recognized the cat I was holding, had seen it come through their yard on several occasions, and had broken up several hissing contests between it and their two cats, Eisenhower and Truman (the Dolans were political science buffs).

But it was not their cat.

*   *   *

19

I didn't know the people at the last house on the right side. I knocked on the door and a girl in her mid-20's answered. Her hair was parted in the middle, dividing the left side, which was black and almost shoulder length, from the pink right side, which was cut about as short as the length of a man's beard after three days of not shaving. She had a ring in her left nostril and a tattoo on her right forearm.

"Hi," I said. "I'm from . . ."

"Cool cat," she said.

"Yeah, she is. I'm . . ."

"What's its name?"

"I don't know. That's why . . ."

"With all the buff coloring in her coat I'd call it Buffy."

"Not a bad idea," I said. "But, see, the reason I'm here is to . . . "

"Wait minute," she said. "Are you one of those gospel guys?"

"Am I what?"

"I bet you are. I bet you're one of those door-to-door gospel guys and you're using this poor cat just to warm up the conversation, huh?"

"What? No, I . . . "

"Yeah, right. Get people talking, get all cozy and stuff, then you hit us up for donations or give us the hard sell to join your little group, huh? You're a scam! How come you don't have some kid with you who's memorized the entire Old Testament or a little monkey playing an accordion? Yeah, that's it! Why don't you go find a monkey and teach him how to play some gospel tune on his accordion, you pervert. Now get lost," she shouted.

Then she slammed the door in my face and the cat's behind.

I whispered into the cat's ear, "Even if you lived here, I'd never let you go back."

I hurried across the street, the cat bouncing on my left shoulder

* * *

The house on the corner was occupied by a Bulgarian seamstress who worshipped Marilyn Monroe and had a dog named Gladys who, if left unleashed, would roam the neighborhood in search of a front yard in which to take a crap. Whenever I saw Gladys she was always crapping. It was a puzzle. Did Gladys just crap a lot which is why I always saw her crapping, or did she hold it when she was in her own yard and then crap when she was in someone else's yard, like mine, which is the only time I would ever see her?

I don't trust Gladys and I'm very suspicious of her Bulgarian owner. The two of them belong in a cheap apartment above a butcher shop in East Berlin.

"No, eet iz nutt my puzzeecot," the Bulgarian seamstress said when I asked if the cat was hers. "I do nutt own cots," she added. "Zey make me eetch."

*   *   *

The next house had a "For Rent" sign in the window. I stood in front of the gated walkway and looked around the yard for signs of cat domesticity. A water bowl, a food dish, maybe some left over mouse parts. Nothing.

I wondered if the people who had lived here and were now gone had left the cat behind, as if she were a mattress too big to pack, or was something unwanted, like a nasty green thing growing in the refrigerator, and was easiest dealt with by closing the door and walking away.

"Oh, the hell with it," the voice echoed in the almost empty house. "We got to get GOIN'! The frig is staying here because it's a piece of junk and because it's a piece of junk that green thing is growin' in there. So let's GO already! I want to get this U-haul back before they close. Otherwise we got to pay for two days!"

"Where's the cat? Is she in the truck?"

He's thinking who cares about that pain-in-the-ass cat. "Yeah, she's in the truck. Let's go."

"Are you sure? I don't see her."

"She's in back somewhere. Close the door. Here we go."

As I stood outside the house, still holding the cat and looking inside a front window, I could picture the slime bag, the one who lied about the cat, jumping into the rental truck, slamming the driver's door shut and driving away, knowing damn straight that there was no cat inside that truck.

I was getting a little upset when I realized my fantasies were out of control. I had never met the previous tenants. I didn't know if they had ever owned this cat, another cat, dog, child, whatever.

I just didn't like the idea of a slime bag getting away with something.

21

The house was now vacant and had the feel of a once prosperous department store now gone bankrupt. There was no one to ask where the colognes were so I could get a free squirt.

So the cat and I moved on.

* * *

After passing a vacant lot, the cat and I stopped in front of a type of house that seems to exist in quite a few neighborhoods of the world. It's the house that the WEIRD OLD WOMAN lives in, the one that little kids cross the street to avoid getting too close to because of the WEIRD OLD WOMAN, the one whose door you should never knock upon because, once opened, there in the doorway, looking you right in the eyes, would stand the WEIRD OLD WOMAN.

And guess what? This house had such a woman: Hazel Morris.

Hazel lived by herself and rarely left the house. A pulled window shade covered every window. You couldn't see in, but you knew that somehow Hazel could see out. The front yard had no lawn, only weeds that were tall and thick and softly swayed in a breeze like wheat in a Kansas prairie.

If Hazel ever entered her house in a contest of houses least likely to be approached by a 7-year-old on Halloween night, hers would easily place in the top three.

To give you an idea of Hazel's brand of weirdness, one summer night a couple of years ago, Glen, our next door neighbor, called me to say that if I looked out our living room window across the street to Hazel's house, I would see her hunched down behind a garbage can by the side of her house with a gun in her hand.

I looked out our front window and Glen was right. There was Hazel with a gun in her right hand. In her left hand she held a fly swatter.

I called the cops.

When asked what she was doing by one of the officers, Hazel told them she was getting ready to drill one of the aliens who lived in her basement and sometimes set off her car alarm in the middle of the night with their comings and goings which was really getting irritating.

"What about the fly swatter, ma'am?" an officer said. "What's that for?"

"Are you trying to be funny?" Hazel said. "It's for all these damn flies.

Upon careful inspection of the premises, the policemen verified the existence of several flies but failed to uncover even one alien. Consequently, Hazel was allowed to keep her fly swatter but relieved of her handgun, and then taken for a very smooth ride in a large police cruiser to Los Gatos Community Hospital where she was kept for 24-hour observation.

She was interviewed by a psychiatrist who found her stubborn and loud with "eccentric tendencies," but, in his opinion, was otherwise apparently normal. She asked for, and received, another smooth ride home by one of the nice young officers who had brought her to the hospital the previous day.

I saw the police car pull up in front of Hazel's house. Hazel sat attentively in the passenger seat as the police officer spoke to her. It looked like he was giving her a litany of instructions. Probably something like "Now remember . . .," "And please don't ever . . .," "So in the event that . . ." Hazel just sat there and looked at the young officer like he was a box of dirt.

Finally Hazel got out of the car, and as the officer drove away, she raised her arm slightly in a half-hearted wave. She walked up the steps to her front door, then went over to a flower pot that sat in a corner of her front porch. She reached in and pulled something out of the flower pot which she dusted off with a handkerchief. She then leaned over her porch railing, looked directly at one of the basement windows, and said "I'm not done with you bastards yet."

Hazel had no children and no husband, but she was the type who could easily have 23 cats living with her, permanently housebound, forever forced to share litter boxes and food bowls, pretending to be content with a 1/23rd ownership of Hazel's Animal Kingdom in exchange for an occasional pat on the head.

I didn't really want to talk to her, but I had to ask Hazel if the cat on my shoulder belonged to her.

I walked up the steps to Hazel's front door. I saw the flower pot over in the corner of the porch. It seemed harmless enough. I knocked on the front door. Waited about 30 seconds. No answer. I knocked again. I saw a hand grab the side of the window shade in the front door window. Then the hand pulled the shade away from the window to make room for the other body parts that soon followed. First there was a nose, then an eye, then an ear with a large lower lobe, over which flowed lots of grey-

23

black hair. I was a witness to a slow motion Hazel appearance. She opened the door a crack.

"So it's you again, Sonny. What do you want?" she said.

(Me again? I hadn't talked to the woman in six months.)

"I was wondering if this cat might be yours, Hazel," I said.

Her eyes moved from my face to the cat.

"Nope. It ain't mine," she said.

"Well, that's O.K., then. I was just wondering."

I got ready to turn around and leave. I've never felt comfortable around Hazel. She was abrupt and cantankerous and suspicious, and generally preferred to keep to herself, unless she had a problem with you, and then you were in for it.

"But I know this cat," she said.

That got my attention.

"Did you say that you know this cat?" I said.

"Yep. I've seen her around. She's a neighborhood wanderer and yammerer. Talks all the time, otherwise I'd take her in. But she talks too much. I don't like too much talking. From humans or cats. Dogs I don't like at all."

Her last sentence was spoken with added emphasis, not so much to point out her dislike for dogs, but to indicate our chat was now over.

"Thanks for your time, Hazel. I'll be going now," I said.

I turned and headed down the steps. I was wondering what I was going to do next with the cat. Hazel was probably right. Most likely the cat was a stray, either lost or abandoned, that had settled into our neighborhood and was surviving off of handouts and whatever it managed to scrounge up or catch.

I thought Hazel had closed the door, ending our conversation, when I heard: "Are you going to keep the cat?"

I looked back up at Hazel who had come outside and was standing on her front porch.

"I don't think so," I said. "My wife and I don't really want any pets."

"If you keep her can you remember something?"

"What's that?" I asked.

"She likes fresh chicken. Don't much like milk."

"How do you know that, Hazel ?" I asked.

24

But Hazel had turned around and started to go back inside her house. Before she closed the door, without bothering to look at me, Hazel said over her shoulder, "Just remember about the other, Sonny."

"The other?" I said.

"She talks too much."

Feeling Four-Feet-In-The-Air Good

Still carrying the cat, I walked back across the street to our house. I pushed the gate open with my hip and entered the front yard. I set the cat down in the middle of the walkway that led to the front door steps. The cat started sniffing the walkway and walking clockwise in a vaguely circular manner, then it reversed itself, and went counter-clockwise, all the while sniffing, sniffing, sniffing.

If I had known that concrete could smell that good, I'd have tried to inhale some myself.

Then the cat lowered the left side of her face onto the walkway, let her body flop down, and proceeded to roll on her back. All four legs went up in the air. She rolled from side to side, and as she rolled she also wriggled her body with a lot of enthusiasm, as if she was finally scratching a previously unreachable itch.

In a few seconds, she stopped rolling around and came to rest on her right side. Lying in the warm afternoon sun, she had her eyes closed and her mouth slightly open, with the tip of her tongue sticking out.

She went from flopping and flipping to napping. Just like that.

John, Next Door

John, who lived next door to us on the side opposite Glen and Muriel, came out of his house and saw me standing over the cat which was lying on our walkway.

He stuck his head over the ivy hedge that separated our houses and said, "Hey, whatchya got there?"

"A mystery cat," I said. "She showed up a few days ago, but we don't know who she belongs to 'cause she doesn't have a collar. I've checked with some of the neighbors, and so far nobody's claimed her."

"Oh, she's been around more than just the last few days," John said. "I've seen her before."

"You have? Where?" I said.

"Walking through my back yard, crossing the street down at the end of the block. You know, here and there. I don't know who she belongs to either. She's probably a stray," John said.

John and I looked at the cat, curled up and cat-napping. She made lying on the sidewalk look comfortable.

"How about it, John," I said. "You want a cat?"

"No, thanks. I'm not interested in having any pets," John said. John was a bachelor at that time. I think he preferred a quiet, solitary lifestyle. Years later, a niece moved in with him and she had a cat. Then the niece moved out and the cat stayed. Then John got married to a woman with a cat so the first cat went back to the niece who also got married and decided to get yet another cat. But at that time, neither John nor I had the ability to foresee these respective futures, so we continued to discuss the cat and the cat continued to lie on the walkway.

"But, you know, I like this cat, even if it did almost give me a heart attack one time," John said.

"What happened?" I said.

"Well, I guess she came into the house when I had the doors open, and decided to stay. Must have found a cozy spot somewhere and fell asleep." John liked to open both his front door and the door that opened into his house from the garage and play classical music on the stereo in the living room while he worked on his old Porsche or cleaned his yard.

"I made dinner, watched a little TV, and went to bed. In the middle of the night, I felt this big THUD that shook my bed and woke me. I didn't know what had happened. First I thought it was an earthquake and maybe something had fallen on the bed. Then I thought I was being attacked! The whole bed jiggled like somebody had jumped on it. And somebody DID! It was THAT CAT," John said, pointing at the cat accusingly, as if the cat had gotten away with something but had now been publicly identified. AH HA! GOTCHA!

"I can see where that could get you up in a hurry," I said.

"I had no idea what had happened," John said.

"Whadya do?" I said.

"I jumped out of bed and turned on the light. I looked at the bed and there was that cat sitting in the middle of the bed, looking at me. At first I was upset with the cat. Then I was glad it was only a cat, you know? The whole thing seems kind of funny now," John said.

Then he added, "Good luck with the cat."

Intersecting Futures

As John disappeared behind the hedge, Cindy came up our driveway carrying flowers she was going to plant in the box outside our bedroom window.

"So what did you find out?" Cindy asked. "Does she belong to anybody on the street?"

"I don't think so," I said, looking at the cat, which had changed its sleeping position. She had now rolled onto her right side. Her chin was down on her chest, and her front legs were fully extended downward and touching the toes of her hind feet. She looked like a diver in the middle of a perfect swan dive. If there were a cat diving Olympic event, she would have received a 10.0 for form alone.

"Both John and Hazel have seen the cat before and they think she's a stray. Maybe they're right. Maybe she wandered over from somewhere else in town. Or maybe somebody either couldn't keep her or didn't want her anymore and dumped her on our street."

Cindy reached down to pet the cat. She stroked her forehead and then scratched her chin. Purring and content, the cat, with its eyes closed and chin stuck out for better accessibility for the scratcher, looked like she would be delighted to stay in that position for the rest of the day.

"What do you think we should do now?" Cindy said.

"Well, I suppose we could put up a few posters with her description around town, give our phone number and see if anybody calls."

"Yeah, that's a good idea."

"While we're doing that we should check around town for any 'lost cat' signs. If she does belong to someone, maybe they're trying to find her."

"I could call the humane society and see if anybody's inquired about a part Siamese, part tabby cat."

"But what'll we do if we don't find her owners?" Cindy said.

The two of us looked down at the cat. She lifted her head up, glanced back over her shoulder, and looked at us.

"I don't want to take her to the humane society," Cindy said. "You know what they'll do with her if nobody adopts her."

Cindy looked at me.

I looked at the cat.

The cat looked at Cindy.

The three of us were at a crossroads of intersecting futures.

"O.K.," I said. "We'll put some 'found cat' signs around town and look for any 'lost cat' signs, but what do we do with her in the meantime?"

I looked at Cindy.

Cindy looked at the cat.

The cat looked at me.

The intersection suddenly felt crowded and the light was about to change. Somebody had to do something.

I had an idea and went to the back of the house, leaving Cindy and the cat staring at each other in the front yard.

I looked under the back stairs, in the basement, and finally found what I wanted in the garage: a large box and an old oval shaped area rug that I used for laying on when I changed the oil in our car. I cut off the four top flaps of the box, then took the box and rug up the back stairs to the back porch and laid the box on its side up against the house. I put the rug inside, and presto, a perfect kitty condo! A three-sided cat-friendly shelter with a roof overhead, an easy-access entrance, and nice wall-to-wall carpeting. So what were a few oil stains?

"But will she use it?" Cindy said as she stood at the bottom of the back stairs. She had brought the cat around back and was holding it in her arms.

"I have no idea," I said. "Let's put her in the box and see what she does."

Cindy came up the stairs with the cat and placed her in front of the box. The cat entered the box slowly, cautiously, sniffing the rug, looking and sniffing at each of the four corners of the box. Then, facing outward, she sat down on the middle of the rug, looked up at the two of us and went "Mmweek."

"There you go. She likes it," I said.

30

As we stood on the back porch, I felt a sense of pride in my spur-of-the-moment creativity and our good deed about to be done. Here was a homeless cat who now had shelter, soft bedding, and, of course, we'd get some cat food for it. I was about to reach down and pet the cat when it suddenly leaped from the box, sprinted down the back stairs, and disappeared into the bushes and trees that formed the lower part of our back yard.

"Then again," I said. "Maybe she likes the street life better."

One Found, Four Lost

The next morning Cindy and I decided to put up flyers describing the cat which we had last seen diving over a juniper bush in our back yard. We both felt she would eventually return. If not for the homemade cat box shelter, then surely she'd find the generous plate of cat food we were planning on leaving outside next to the box on the back porch.

Our flyers were simple. On six sheets of standard size typing paper we wrote: Cat Found. Part Siamese, Part Tabby. Female. Apprx. 1 year old. Call Vic or Cindy, 354-8247. I figured six flyers were enough. A greater number would not exert a stronger influence on fate or change anyone's mind regarding cat ownership responsibilities.

I put the flyers and a roll of masking tape in my backpack, then I hopped on my 26-year-old Schwinn bicycle for a cruise around downtown Los Gatos. I looked for telephone poles and light posts in busy pedestrian areas that were up to the job of shouting to passersby:

> "Hey! You!
> Is this your CAT?
> If it is, get over to our place
> and PICK IT UP! NOW!
> and don't let it get lost in the FUTURE!"

As I rode my bike through town and picked spots for our "Cat Found" signs, I noticed other flyers that people had put up. One read:

> "Lost. Brown Dog. Name: Brownie. If found, don't bother calling him by his name. He don't come. Ever. Call me instead. John at 354-6289."

Another one said:

"Lost. Black and white female cat named Bibbers. 11 years old. Wearing flea collar and name tag. Reward offered. Peggy or Bill 356-8752. If you're tempted to keep her, please remember, we've loved her for 11 years."

One was about a bird:
"Lost again. Blue and white parakeet. Answers to "Pretty Boy." Very vocal. Always wants out of the house, but can never find his way back in. Will sit on an extended finger. Don't let him near your ears. Max 354-1058."

And:

"Lost. A great basketball shoe. Size 9. For the left foot. A black hightop with black laces. If you find this shoe, call Jerome at 395-0929. I'll buy you a beer.

I couldn't believe that Jerome would put up a sign announcing that he had lost a shoe, for godsakes. I mean, it's a shoe we're talking about. A lost shoe does not warrant a sign advertising its disappearance on a prime telephone pole location, and this one happened to be by the newspaper racks in front of the Baker's Square restaurant where I always go to get our Sunday newspaper. It was a great spot! Lots of foot traffic! A perfect suburban mélange of pie-eaters, skateboarders, cops on breaks, joggers. A chair with a view of such a corner could easily replace network television programming.

I pulled down the lost shoe sign and put up the last of our "Cat Found" signs in the lost shoe sign space.

I also made a mental note that when I went to the gym on the following Saturday to be sure to return Jerome's shoe.

It was a long story.

Nobody Called

Over the next few days the phone didn't ring with a breathless voice on the other end asking how in the world did we ever find Miss Whatever and is she all right and I've been looking everywhere and where is she now and you live where? Oh, my GOSH! How did she ever get way over THERE?

There was none of that.

The phone never rang producing anyone searching for a blue-eyed, light and dark brown streaked and spotted cat with fat white paws and really soft fur.

Nobody called.

We waited and wondered to whom did the cat belong?

Did something tragic and fatal happen to her guardians? Then, by chance and circumstance, did the cat amazingly escape disaster only to find itself miles from home?

Did she belong to a forgetful little old lady who let her cat out of the house one day only to remember to look for it about a week later?

Were her guardians abducted and now rotting in a foreign jail pleading with their captors because they had to go home to feed their cat?

We never found out.

Because nobody called.

Not even anyone wanting to get a free cat. Then again, cats aren't exactly in short supply since too many people are too stupid to get their cats fixed. They let their cats reproduce like rabbits and then their solution is either to leave the litter of kittens behind the nearest supermarket, or move to Nebraska when the cats aren't looking.

Nobody called.

Not even Jerome to complain about his "lost shoe" sign being taken down.

Birds

During the time of nobody calling about the cat, thoughts like stray birds flew into my brain. Their wings fluttered and flapped against my temples as they looked for a way out.

Where does a homeless cat go during the long hours of the day when human kindness is not there to pet its head and say soothing words and refill its water bowl?

Do homeless cats sleep at night, or do they spend the dark hours anxiously sitting and staring into the darkness with great vigilance pretending to be unafraid of shadowy movements and uncertain sounds?

I began to worry about this cat that had entered our lives. Then again, it wasn't my cat. It wasn't my responsibility. It certainly wasn't the first wandering stray cat that we had seen in our six years in the neighborhood, which didn't include the previous three years we spent renting a house two blocks away.

I remembered one cat, a puffy black and white, Cindy and I had christened "Old Tom." He used to come walking by every three or four days, his fur matted and dirty, giving us a glance as he passed by, never looking directly at us but taking in everything with the quickest of peeks out of the corners of his eyes. Never wanting to get too close, he always maintained a respectful distance. Somewhere along his life's journey he had learned to be distrustful of the human species, so dispassionate fleeting looks were as much as he was inclined to give.

I'd be raking leaves or washing the car or sitting on the back steps watching the squirrels race around our neighbor's gigantic oak tree, when Old Tom would come along around the corner of our house. As he slowly shuffled by, he moved with a steady rhythm that kept him going ever forward, as if he never wanted to give the impression that he was coming to stay in another cat's territory. Whenever I tried to move closer to him, to try to pet him or offer food, Old Tom would pick up the pace of his shuffle and move just a bit quicker, never allowing his protective safety, the distance between us, to be diminished in any way.

Old Tom always seemed to be well fed. He had a belly on him. He probably got by on working the little old ladies circuit in town. They are a clandestine and loosely organized bunch, those ladies, who seem to delight in providing surreptitious snacks for anything four-legged and freely roaming. I wondered if in the days of the Wild West little old ladies would sneak off in early twilight, just after dinner, with baskets of hay and fruit, tip-toeing into canyons to feed wild mustangs, burros and bobcats, and what the heck, if an occasional Indian wanted an apple, well, that might have been O.K., too.

Old Tom had sad, droopy eyes and a gentle countenance. I never heard or saw him hissing at another cat. It was almost as if he felt cat fights were a waste of time. He never begged. He never bothered. He just slowly moved in time until his time was over and then I never saw him again.

I thought about this new cat and I thought about Old Tom and I thought about all the cats on the planet that didn't have a place to call home. I wondered how many of them there were.

Then I thought about this new cat some more.

A Conversation Between Patio Security Guards

Inside our house, Cindy and I stood side by side at the back window. We were both looking down at the patio.

"So what do we do now?" I said.

"I don't know," Cindy said.

Then we didn't say anything more for a while. We continued looking down at the patio as if we were patio security guards, developing the ability to stare without blinking for considerable lengths of time.

"Do you think we should do something?" Cindy said.

"What else can we do?" I said, still looking at the patio, noticing that the patio tiles looked just like they did the day before, realizing that tomorrow they probably would look pretty much like they did today.

"You know she's out there somewhere," one of us said.

"Mm-hmm," the other one said.

"She's going to show up sooner or later."

"Mm-hmm."

"She needs a home."

"Mm-hmm."

"Do we know anybody who wants a cat?"

"Like who?"

"There must be somebody."

"Who?"

"How about Dave?"

"He likes birds."

"Jerome."

"I don't think so."

"Marie and John."

"Two dogs and one cat is enough. She's told me."

"Andrew and Bryan."

"They just adopted another cat. They're at their limit."

"Phil and Monika."

"They're poodle people. And they have a new grandchild."

Then there was silence as our mind's eyes scanned lists of names of people we knew who were candidates for cat adoption.

A minute went by during which no name was mentioned.

A second minute of silence followed. The uninterrupted patio viewing was excellent.

In the spirit of an oft-noted phenomenon, which is: the third item in a series is frequently the one most notable, the one that works, the one that is the answer, it was the third pensive minute that gave voice to a shocking question that burst the silence like the BOOM of a thunderclap.

To this day we're not certain whose voice, Cindy's or mine, uttered three words that exploded in our brains. We were showered with debris from the blast. All around us lay broken bits of unspoken thoughts and partially completed sentences

We were stunned!

The voice had asked,

"What about us?"

The Advantages Of Renting Cats

One obstacle stood in the way of our adopting a pet. We didn't want to.

It's not that we didn't love animals. We did. We just preferred liking somebody else's cat or dog. It was so much easier that way.

We loved going for walks in the neighborhood and finding a cat sitting in its yard waiting for something to happen. We'd stop our stroll and stand within the cat's line of sight. When the cat spotted us, its almond shaped eyes would go round with curiosity and excitement and it would come loping over to check us out. New people! New smells! How fun!

We'd pet its head, scratch its belly, gently rub its ears between our fingertips. If a stalky weed or long twig was handy, we'd grab it and dangle it in front of the cat's nose. The cat would clutch and claw at the dangly thing until it successfully ripped it out of our hands, demonstrating yet one more time the quickness and cunning that allows cats to be forever superior to all dangly things.

It was wonderful!

Sometimes someone would see us fooling around with their cat, and the person would come out of the house. They might have been concerned that we were some sort of demented, middle-aged catnappers. But we always explained that we were neighbors and how we really loved cats. We also liked dogs and birds but enjoying cats was our specialty. Then they'd let us mess with the cat some more.

That's why we never wanted to have a pet of our own.

Just a casual walk in the neighborhood produced great animal entertainment, and we didn't have to watch the newspaper for pet food sales, or buy 17 different kinds of flea collars hoping to find one that worked, or have our bedroom carpet turn into a Disneyland for fleas since no flea collar really works that well, or pay vet bills, or ever have to wonder how in hell did that cat ever get up there, or clean up hair balls, or replace shredded furniture.

So why should we bother to have our own cat, and have to do all that stuff, when you could rent a cat from your neighbors for free?

Still, there was the matter of this cat that needed a home.

Cats and dogs do not do well on their own in modern environments. For these guys, the odds of making it safely across a busy road were about as good as winning a state lottery. Their paws were not made for grasping garbage can lids, so scrounging for food in alleyways was minimally productive. Their lack of reading skills hindered their ability to read street signs – useful for a cat when it's roamed too far and become lost, or might need to find a veterinary hospital to check in for some repair work.

Clearly, cats and dogs need humans to provide a home for food, shelter, and fun times.

But, as previously stated, we had no interest in becoming pet owners.

No! Nunca! Nyet! No way was that boat gonna float in our pond.

We loved animals, and yes, this cat was pretty and soft and furry, but we just didn't want to own a pet.

So I came up with a compromise plan that I thought should work for all parties involved.

"Why don't we do this," I said. "Let's get this cat a collar and name tag and we'll put our phone number on the tag. That way, if she ever gets in a jam, needs something like medical attention, hopefully someone would find her, spot the number on her tag, and call us and we could help out. Otherwise, she could be the neighborhood cat. Maybe everybody on the street would take part in taking care of her."

Cindy wasn't sold on the neighborhood cat idea. She didn't think that a stray cat wandering from house to house was going to be consistently fed and cared for. Ultimately, this cat needed a permanent home. The more I thought about it, I agreed with Cindy. But we both thought the collar with our phone number was a good idea. That way, she'd at least have us for help in an emergency situation.

Then Cindy said, "We should name her."

"Why should we name her?" I said.

"She's going to have a collar. She's going to have a name tag. She might as well have a name, so we can call her by name instead of saying, 'Hey, there's the cat.'"

"O.K.," I said. "What should we call her?"

Orsy the Kid Doesn't Work

Choosing a name for a cat is no small matter.

The cat is going to have its name for a long time, so it's gotta be right.

It's like getting a custom-made suit. It should be a good fit, not too tight across the shoulders, not too loose in the bottom.

Hey! A name is important! A good name can help make a mark, a bad name can destroy a promising future.

What if Mr. and Mrs. Hickock had named their son Orson, not an uncommon name in the 1800s? Do you think that Wild Orson Hickock would have had a niche in Western legend?

Would Pat Garrett have had any interest in tracking down and shooting someone named Orsy the Kid?

Not a chance.

So Cindy and I had a big job in determining a good name for this cat.

Cindy said she was going to the local pet store to get a collar and name tag for the cat. Meanwhile, I was supposed to come up with some names.

Buffy? Tuffy? Rose Milianti?

Cindy returned from the pet store with a blue cat collar which had a small metal name tag hanging from it. The name tag was blank. It was up to us to fill it.

"Not that I've known a lot of cats in my time," I said, "but that cat talks more than any cat I've ever seen. The way she chatters constantly, I think we should call her Muttering Marge."

"Not bad. Or how about Chatty Cathy?" Cindy added. "Just like the talking doll."

Then we got on a roll.

"Since she basically lives in this neighborhood, we could name her after our street, Edelen, and call her Edie," Cindy said.

"The girl down the street thought she should be called Buffy after her coloring," I said.

"She seems fearless and street tough. Like a Tuffy."

"How about Wanda the Wanderer?"

"Or we could give her a good full Italian name, like Rose Milianti."

We were acting stupid. None of those names were right. I could picture cats with those names and this cat did not fit in that photo album.

I imagined Marge and Cathy and Edie as slovenly cats who didn't know a gopher hole from a key hole. Buffy was grossly overweight and shoud have been called Chubs. Tuffy had one ear all chewed up and fur that looked like a worn brillo pad. Wanda needed to live in a monastery or some large stucco building. Rose Milianti might not even have been a cat. Rose might have been a ferret.

I'm like that with names. I can't remember names at all. But I know what names go with which bodies. Taking into account shape and size and unique characteristics and such, I'm an ace with names. I'm good with human nicknames, too.   I should have been a pediatrician specializing in naming difficult children and vagabond cats.

The authoritative pediatrician in me spoke up.

"These names aren't any good for this cat," I said.

"So what should we call her then?" Cindy said.

"I don't know," I said. "Let's decide the next time we see her."

We didn't have long to wait.

A Sedona Moment of Vector Inspiration

Two days later, we saw her walking on the sidewalk in front of our house. We heard the cat before we saw her.

She was muttering to herself, like an old lady who couldn't remember where she had parked her car and was getting frustrated because if she didn't find that car soon and get home she was going to miss her favorite soap opera.

What did we hear?

We did not hear your traditional "mee-ow" cat sound, or its distant cousin, a "ree-ow" made by cats too lazy to flex their lips properly.

She kind of went "mmreeak," then "oohrk?" with an inflection at the end as if she was asking a question, then she took a deep breath which made her sides billow out and made a final comment: "reek."

She passed our front gate, continuing to yammer sporadically, and went over to our neighbor's driveway and lay down in the shade cast by a large maple tree.

Looking back over her shoulder, she looked at the two of us and said "yowrf," then laid her head down as if to take an afternoon snooze.

"There she is," Cindy said. "Now's the time for us to come up with a good name for her. Let's go over and see her."

We went out our front gate and over to our neighbor's driveway and walked up to the cat. She opened her eyes to look at us and flipped her head up in a "Hey, how's it going?" acknowledgment and went "murk?"

"You know, for the talkingest cat around, I've never heard her say anything that resembles a good, clear 'meow,' " I said. "Sometimes she sounds like a crow, other times she sounds like a small bird with something caught in its windpipe. But she never sounds like a cat."

44

"Why don't you help us?" Cindy said to the cat. "Since you like to talk so much, why don't you tell us what you would like to be called?"

The cat knew it was being addressed and responded to Cindy. It went "eeek." It was a half-hearted and distant "eeek," coming from a warm dopiness that enveloped her as she lay in full sunlight on the concrete driveway.

The cat, which had been lying on its left side, looked up at us, then rolled over onto its right side. As she rolled, she opened her mouth as if to say something but nothing came out. She seemed to be drifting into a sun-induced stupor.

I said, "I think I heard her say 'eeek.' I think she wants to be called 'eeek.'" Cindy, lost in concentration, didn't respond. The cat was on its side, napping.

There we three were once again. Only this time there was no exchange of looks. The cat had entered dreamland. Its eyes were now closed and her breathing had slowed. One minute "eeeking," the next minute sleeping.

"You're right about this cat," Cindy said. "It mutters and yammers, but it doesn't meow. It just seems to . . . ."

That's when it happened.

Cindy paused in the middle of her statement, and a peaceful energy floated around us giving us the feeling that questions were going to be answered. Decisions were about to be made. You could tell that correct things were about to happen. It was a Sedona Moment of Vector Inspiration.

Cindy got excited!

It was a moment of discovery and celebration!

It was like traveling back in time to 1848 and dipping your hand in the creek at Sutter's Mill and pulling out that bright, shiny nugget of gold!

"I think I've got it," Cindy said. "The way she sounds when she talks. Why don't we call her . . . Squeeky?"

Squeeky?

Squeeky.

Perfect.

"Hey, Squeeky"

With the name decided, Cindy went to the pet store to get the name tag imprinted. She came back holding the blue collar from which dangled the silvery metallic tag, the name "Squeeky" visible on one side; the other side showed our phone number.

I liked the look of the tag, shaped like a shield of armor. It looked like something a cat that cut her teeth on the greater part of the outdoors would be proud to wear.

The cat, now named Squeeky, was still lying in the neighbor's driveway. She looked like a furry oil slick on the concrete. As we walked up to her she went "reewirk?"

We put the collar on her and she didn't fuss or squirm or wriggle at all. It didn't bother her. I figured she must have had a collar at some earlier time and she was used to having something around her neck. Or maybe she just liked it, the collar being a sharp blue color and the name tag being a cool shape.

With the collar on she officially became Squeeky. She was the cat with no name no more.

Now I had to get her used to her name.

So I walked about 10 feet away from Squeeky and crouched down and sat on my heels like a baseball catcher and called out to her.

I said, "Hey, Squeeky."

She turned her head toward me, looked at me for a second, then put her head back down.

So I tried again.

I said, "Hey, Squeeky."

Once more she turned her head towards me while she continued to lie on the driveway.

I thought that was amazing! She responded to her name! What an intelligent cat!

I started to go back in the house and then I thought of something else to try. Cupping my hands around my mouth, I hollered, "Hey, lampshade."

She turned her head towards me.

"Forget it," I said. "The tag's paid for and the letters won't fit."

So What's to Eat?

I figured this cat, now named Squeeky, sitting on our walkway, looking up at me, had just about everything.

Looks: Pretty mottled colors. Interwoven browns and whites. She looked like a bird's nest made out of fleece.

Shape: Classic cat body. Nice tail.

A home: Our neighborhood, our street, and on occasion, our yard.

"What more could a cat ask for?" I asked out loud and philosophically.

Then I looked at Squeeky.

It occurred to me that as interested as she may have been in her new blue collar and a piece of jewelry which displayed her newly given name, she might have been more interested and in greater need of something more basic.

Like something to eat.

Service For One

I got on my old Schwinn bike and rode over to the supermarket to get some cat food. It was a learning experience.

Of the dry variety of cat food, the store had lots of choices. They came in small boxes, medium-sized boxes, and large plastic jugs with handles on them. Assorted cat treats in small packages were available, too. They were like candy bars for cats.

Then I had to pick a particular flavor. It's not like you can simply buy generic cat food. There were boxes of fish flavored nuggets, next to beef flavored crunchems, next to chicken-flavored things, next to boxes advertising a mix of flavors.

Then there was moist food to consider with just as many flavor choices.

These came mostly in small cans, although there were some soup can sizes of moist food as well. I figured they were for large cats. Squeeky was a medium-sized cat.

I picked a small box of ocean whitefish & tuna flavored dry cat food that had a picture of a cat licking its chops with an agreeable look on its face.

When I got home I poured some of the food into a small plastic bowl and put it on the back porch. I also put out a bowl of water.

That was mid-afternoon.

By early evening, a little before sundown, Squeeky came sauntering across the back patio. She was strolling along peacefully and checking things out. *"Hm-mm. Flowers. Bugs. Oh look, a leaf just fell in the driveway. But what's that up on that back porch in those two bowls? What is that incredibly dee-licious smell coming from that area?"*

Squeeky never hesitated.

She willingly and trustingly walked up those steps liked she owned them and went to that bowl and crunched her way through every morsel of cat food.

49

After eating, she turned to the bowl of water and had a good long drink.

When she finished drinking, she lifted her head up and looked into the house through one of the window panes in the back door.

She saw the two of us standing there watching her and grinning, like we were the proud parents of a child that just took its first steps.

Then Squeeky walked down the steps, took a left turn and disappeared around the side of the garage into our neighbor's yard.

The Plan

With placement of the food and water bowls on the back porch, our house had now become an official way station for Squeeky.

We had become a one cat "safe house," a sanctuary for this night rider who at some point during her evening meanderings might need a quick refueling during the dark hours, or a place to hang during the daytime when the angle of sunlight was perfect and the daylight warmth provided a blanket of security.

At this time, Cindy and I had no greater expectations of Squeeky other than an occasional sighting. Our house was not going to be her permanent home. It was supposed to be a pit stop, a roadside rest area, a Howard Johnson-For-Squeeky open 24 hours a day, every day for whatever she might need, "BUT DON'T THINK YOU LIVE HERE, CAT. GOT THAT?"

"Just because we're nice people and don't want to see any harm come to an indigent beast such as you does NOT mean we will be taken ADVANTAGE OF!"

"We are in control of our lives."

"We read Consumer Reports."

"We watch the educational channel on TV. Sometimes."

"We have fulfilling lives to lead which is why no kids, cats, dogs, other people, or other people's furniture are allowed here for any time span longer than the time it takes to make and eat a bowl of popcorn."

"You will always be welcome to visit us, Squeeky, but when playtime's over . . . VAMOOSE!"

That was the plan.

Until One Day

The plan worked well for a while.

Squeeky would show up during the morning, eat, drink, and leave.

Later in the day, or perhaps the next day, she'd show up, eat, drink, and occasionally snooze, either curled up on the back porch, or nestled in a bunch of leaves under the hedge that lined our front yard.

Or it'd be a snack at dinnertime and then off she'd go and spend the night somewhere in the neighborhood. At first we were concerned about her being out all night. Where did she go? Where did she sleep? Was it somewhere indoors? Was someone else in the neighborhood letting her into their house at night? Or did she find a secluded spot under a deck, an overturned box, a pile of leaves, and make that her bedding for the night?

We'd hear the occasional middle of the night cat fight and we'd wonder if Squeeky was involved. She must have had her share of confrontations. But whenever she showed up, she always looked fine. I never saw any signs of warfare on her. A two or three day disappearance never preceded a limping fife and drum return. She was either a peaceful sort. Or a cat who had no trouble taking care of business. So we stopped worrying about her.

Besides, Squeeky never wanted to stick around for any length of time. She usually ate and ran. Sometimes she stayed long enough for us to pet her, watch her roll around on her back, scratch her under her chin, pat her belly, and then she'd split.

Squeeky appeared to be content, and so were we, with our low-maintenance, see-you-now-and-again relationship that seemed to meet everybody's needs.

Until one day.

On that day, Squeeky had shown up as usual, had some bites from her food bowl, and then instead of heading back down the stairs that led to the adventures found in the untamed wilderness that was our neighborhood, she walked up to the lower window panes of the back door and looked in.

And kept looking in.

I was inside, and as I happened to walk by the back door, I glanced down and saw Squeeky. I was a few feet away from the door. When she saw me she meowed, or better said, squeeked a greeting. I opened the door and looked down at Squeeky and said "Hello there. What's up, Squeeky?"

I expected her to say something, allow me to pat her head, then head down the back steps.

She was only partially true to form. She muttered a greeting, accepted my patting of her head . . .

then came inside.

A Nose With No Wings

Squeeky entered the house cautiously and v-e-r-y s-l-o-w-l-y.

She was not going to be anybody's unsuspecting target for cheap thrills. If this exploration led to an unsavory situation, such as rounding a corner and coming face to face with the Snapping Jaws From Hell, she was prepared to disappear REAL FAST!

It was a Charlie Chaplinesque slow motion entrance.

First, Squeeky's nose broke the vertical plane of the open doorway. Then her head followed, most reluctantly. But between being pulled by its nose and pushed by its outstretched neck, the head had no choice. It came inside the house.

Squeeky strained mightily to see further into the house without actually bringing her body inside.

I think she would have preferred her nose to sprout wings so she could send it out on a quick fly-over to sniff out the rest of the house. But she was out of luck. She had a wingless nose. She still had to satisfy her innate cat's curiosity, though. She had no choice. She had to come into the house.

As she cautiously moved forward, Squeeky lifted and planted each leg like she was walking through jello. You could almost hear her talking to herself, "*Careful, now, careful, careful, careful.*"

I left the door open. I thought if Squeeky freaked out at something and leaped toward the door, it might be best if the door was open. I didn't want to have to deal with either a broken door or a broken cat.

The first room she entered was the TV room. The TV wasn't on. She paused in mid-stride and looked at the blank TV screen, as if to assess its status, friend or foe? Then she continued, crouching low, into the next room.

Off the TV room there are two doorways. One goes to the second bedroom which Cindy and I converted to a study. The other doorway goes to the kitchen. Squeeky went toward the kitchen.

She stopped in the middle of the kitchen and lifted her head up. I saw her whiskers start to twitch and her tiny nostrils flex. She had entered the Room of Wondrous Smells.

Cindy happened to be at the kitchen counter with a bag of groceries. I said, "Don't move and don't say anything. We are under surveillance."

Squeeky crept through the kitchen and entered the biggest room in the house, the living room. I followed several feet behind. Cindy joined in and followed me. The three of us, in single file, slinked through the living room.

Squeeky sniffed at the sofa and rubbed up on one of its edges. She went up to the coffee table in front of the sofa, circled around it, then walked and sniffed around the two chairs opposite the sofa. After looping around the chairs, Squeeky strolled past our bedroom doorway. She tilted her head sideways, pausing to give the room a cursory inspection, then continued walking and wound up by the front door. She sat down in front of the door, went "squaark?" and looked up at me.

"I think she wants to go out," Cindy said.

"Why does she want to go out?" I said. "She just got here. Besides, how does she know that door leads outside? This is her first time in the house. She should be more careful. That could be the door to the room that holds three wild dogs."

"Somehow I think she's smarter than that," Cindy said.

Cindy opened the front door and Squeeky stood in the doorway and surveyed the front yard. Recognition seemed to cross her face like a thought in a crosswalk. "*I know this place*," her eyes said. "*I've just never seen it from up here before.*"

Squeeky went out and down the front steps like she'd done it a hundred times before.

"You know what I think?" Cindy said.

"What?" I said.

"I think she thinks that she's moved in."

I looked at Squeeky. She had curled up on the walkway leading up to our front door steps. The sun was shining on her. She looked like she didn't have a care in the world.

She looked like she knew it was a good day to be a cat on Edelen Ave. in Los Gatos, California, even if she didn't have wings on her nose.

Cheerios For Cats

Despite coming inside our house for the first time, Squeeky spent the night outside, in her usual terrain. She didn't want to come back and sleep inside.

Just before it got dark, I saw Squeeky eating from her food bowl on the back porch. I opened the back door and said, "Hey, you wanna come inside?" Squeeky lifted her head up and looked at me. Then she went back to eating. When she finished, she sat on the top step and licked her paws and gave herself a proper face cleaning. When she was done with that, she walked down the back steps and disappeared in the bushes that rimmed our backyard.

She expressed no interest in spending the night indoors.

But the next morning, as I made my way into the kitchen to make some coffee, I noticed a familiar pair of ears and eyes framed in the lower right hand corner window of the back door.

When Squeeky saw me her eyes grew round and she immediately started chattering, "rork, reek, areek." Through the closed door it sounded like somebody trying to gargle and do a bird call at the same time.

I opened the door to give her a pat on the head. As I glanced at her food bowl out on the back porch to see if it needed filling, Squeeky stepped over my right foot and strolled purposefully inside. I watched her furry bottom disappear into the kitchen.

Squeeky's food bowl was almost empty, so I grabbed it and brought it inside for a fresh fill.

I came into the kitchen. Squeeky, sitting in the middle of the floor, looked up at me and started talking again. This time she went "reer, reer," closing with "rarr-ra?" The last utterance was her two syllable vocalization with the second syllable pitched upward. It was a question of sorts.

"Yeah, I'm gonna give you some more food," I said, reaching for a box of dry cat food on the kitchen counter.

I filled the food bowl with little round circular things with a hole in the middle of each one. They looked like Cheerios that were altered for cat consumption. I think they took regular Cheerios and sprayed them with something to make them taste like fish or some kind of small rodent. Squeeky liked them.

I place the food bowl next to Squeeky on the kitchen floor and she started wolfing down her Cheerios for cats.

I went back outside and got her water bowl, filled it with fresh water and placed it next to her food.

I sat at the kitchen table, watching her and listening to her eat. She made a crunching noise as she bit into the pieces of dry food that sounded kind of neat. It sounded like she was really enjoying eating those circular things. Nice crisp, crackling, crunching sounds, lips occasionally smackng, more crunching.

It made me hungry so I poured myself a bowl of cereal.

Discovery Of The Blue Shawl

I finished my cereal and Squeeky gulped the last of her food at about the same time. I was sitting at the kitchen table and looked down at her. Squeeky licked her chops a few times and then licked her right paw which she then used to clean her face. I had seen other cats do this paw-licking, face-wiping activity before. But I had never paid close attention to the fact that they were creating wash cloths out of their own paws. Five fingers short of a hand gives rise to that old feline saying: "cleverness is next to cleanliness."

"I suppose you want to go out now," I said.

She was still cleaning her face.

I raised my voice a little.

"Hey, you wanna go out?" I said.

She stopped her cleaning act in mid-stroke. It was like we were playing that kids' game of Freeze Tag and my voice tagged her with her tongue out and now it was stuck on her paw. She was looking up at me with a look that could only be described as one of disgust bordering on unbelievability. Her expression shouted, *"MUST you interrupt me so rudely! I'm doing some SERIOUS CLEANING here!"*

"OK. Whatever," I said. "I'm going to go into the TV room and watch some news. You let me know when you want to go out."

I went into the TV room and sat in the recliner. Besides the TV, there were only two other pieces of furniture in the room, the recliner and a small sofa.

I turned the TV on to watch the local morning news, my usual routine, before I went off to work.

Squeeky walked into the middle of the TV room, sat down, looked at me and went "mmm-MM?" A bit of vocabulary from her I hadn't heard yet. It was a combination question mark and comment.

As I sat in the recliner I had an idea. I pointed to my lap and tapped my right leg and said, "Do you want to come up here?"

"Mmm."

"Why don't you come up here and we can watch the news together?"

Again the "mmm-MM?" with a somewhat puzzled expression on her face.

"Or do you want to go out? Maybe you want to go out."

I got up out of the recliner and walked to the back door, thinking Squeeky would follow me to be let out. But she didn't follow me. She sat in the middle of the floor, not saying anything for a change, and stared at me with those eyes so blue that if you looked at them long enough you could see clouds.

I had another idea. Over one sofa arm we had a neatly folded blue shawl. We used it once in a while for extra warmth in the wintertime when we'd watch TV at night. I picked up the shawl and laid it, still folded, on the sofa. Then I picked up Squeeky. She didn't squirm or wriggle but her eyes were open wide with concern. As I placed her on the shawl, Squeeky was apprehensively checking it out, as if it might be the covering for a trap door that connected to a chute that funneled everything into a cat-shredding machine.

"There," I said. "How's that feel?"

Squeeky looked up at me and then started sniffing every inch of that blue shawl. First, she went in a clockwise direction, once around, twice around, then she reversed herself and went in a counterclockwise direction. This went on for a minute or two, until Squeeky finally sat down in the middle of the shawl. Then she started making a kneading motion with her two front paws. Slowly, but methodically alternating her paws, left-right-left-right. I was fascinated by that. She was really getting into pushing on that shawl. She reminded me of a job I once had as day manager at Me-n-Ed's Pizza Parlor. Every day I used to roll out the dough and prep it for that night's pizza baking. I thought I had a good kneading technique, but Squeeky could have taught me a thing or two. She kind of leaned forward and put her body into it. She was getting that shawl just right.

When she was done, Squeeky curled up into a tight ball, tucked her head down on her chest, covered her nose with her front paws, and started to doze.

I watched all this sitting in the recliner.

59

I had to get ready, shower and such, to go to work. As I stood up to turn off the light in the room, Squeeky drowsily opened one eye over her paws and glanced at me.

"I'm gonna go take a shower so don't get concerned if you don't see anybody for a while. I'll be back to let you out in a little bit," I said.

I didn't have to hurry. Squeeky slept soundly for the next 4 hours and 19 years on that blue shawl.

Moving Day

I didn't realize it at the time, but when Squeeky curled up and went to sleep on that blue shawl, that was pretty much moving day. The food bowl was in. The water bowl was in. Squeeky was in.

"How did this happen," I thought.

I trolled through the waters of my memory and I could not dredge up a conversation between Cindy and myself in which the desires for having a pet were ever expressed.

I could swear that I had never heard Cindy mention the need for acquiring a hamster, ferret, gerbil, bird of any sort, llama, dog, monkey, turtle, fish, pig, pony, reptile . . . or cat.

The only thing I ever wanted to own was a stock that was going to double by next Friday.

And yet . . .

lying on the sofa,

was a cat,

with a collar on its neck,

with a name that WE had given it,

and when it got hungry,

it had food and water laid out in the next room! The only thing missing was a menu board with the day's specials on it.

"What we have we done?" I thought. Were we crazy? Stupid? Had we made a rash decision that we would soon regret?

I thought about Squeeky, the shawl, the food, the water. Although I didn't really want to, I knew what I had to do next.

I got on my bike and rode over to the pet store.

I had realized Squeeky might need a litter box.

Litter Stories

At the pet store I bought a 5 pound bag of litter and a plastic box in which to pour the litter.

I rode home on my bike with the litter bag under my arm and the litter box jammed into my backpack. Along the way, I passed two kids walking along University Ave. Seeing what I was carrying, one of them shouted, "Hey, man. What's the problem? Is your toilet broke?"

Little turds. Thought they were funny. Couple of wits.

But they were just two little turds walking along University Ave.

On my ride home I did have visions of getting up ahead of them and hiding in some bushes, and when they'd pass by I'd reach into that bag of cat litter, grab a fistful and heave it at them, yelling, "Yeah, I miss my toilet but it's kind of fun getting rid of the old litter."

When reality disappoints, imagining can be quite satisfying.

When I got home I put the litter box on the floor right next to the desk in our second bedroom, the office room. I filled the box with about half the bag of litter. It seemed to be about right. Then, it occurred to me that I didn't know how to house-train a cat. There were no instructions on the litter bag for either a cat owner or a cat on how to use the litter in a proper way for maximum utility and minimum malfeasance.

Cindy had never had a pet and she wasn't sure what to do.

I had an Irish Setter puppy for two days as a kid in Illinois. My only memories of him were ripping the bottom of my pants legs on the first day we got him, and on the second day, his leaving a puddle on the kitchen floor. I also remember my mother grabbing King, which is what I named him, and putting him outside. My mother said he was going to have to stay outside until he learned better. He must have been a slow learner because he stayed outside for about a week and then I never saw him any more.

At the time, I wondered what happened to ol' King. I sort of missed his grabbing me by the ankles. My mother just said someday we'd get another dog, which we did, years later. (I think my folks gave King away.)

I was sitting at the desk in the office room and thinking about King and why cats use litter boxes and dogs don't, and wondering what to do about training Squeeky, when Squeeky came walking into the room. Cindy had just let her into the house. Squeeky looked up at me, went "reeork?" and walked up to the litter box. She gave it two good sniffs and proceeded to walk into the box, squatted and peed, like she'd been peeing in that box next to the desk her whole life. She meticulously covered up her pee and created a nice litter mound, as if someday religious artifacts might be found there. Then she went to her blue shawl for a nap.

The thought occurred to me that it wasn't all that difficult to house-train a cat. You just had to know what to do.

Inners And Outers

So the routine began.

When Squeeky wanted to come in, we'd let her in.

If she wanted to go out, we'd let her out.

With very little discussion among the three of us, we all agreed that Squeeky was to be an In-and-Out Cat, which distinguished her from those cats that are solely Inners and those that are mostly Outers.

Your Inners are those felines that are not permitted under any circumstances to venture outdoors. They are typically coddled and spoiled and gain a ridiculous amount of weight because all they do is sleep and eat and sleep some more and when they wake up they panic because they look in their food bowl and all their food is gone.

Inners should be allowed to go outside at least twice a year, perhaps once in the Spring and again in the Fall, to experience two of the great satisfactions of being a cat: (1) peeing on a car tire, and (2) sniffing a car tire that has been peed upon by another cat. To a cat, the blended aroma of rubber and cat pee is intoxicating.

Outer cats look horrible. Their fur is unkempt and matted. They're always itching and scratching because they have fleas. Outer cats are often missing some of their favorite body parts, which have been lost forever in turf wars with other Outers. Survivors of these battles manage to get along with reduced ambition and a more global attitude of tolerance and forgiveness. But they don't really like it.

If Squeeky had been outside for a while and wanted to come in, she'd stick her face in that lower right-hand corner window in the back door and start talking, asking to be let in, and we'd let her in. That is, if we were home and heard her. If we weren't there to let her in, I guess she went away.

There were times when Cindy and I would be gone all day, and whoever was first to come home would immediately go to the back door and see if Squeeky was there, and so many times, sure enough, there she'd be, talking.

I used to wonder: on those occasions when we were both gone for most of the day, if Squeeky showed up at the back door at, say, 10:00 in the morning, and if neither of us showed up until, say, 4:00 in the afternoon, did Squeeky sit at the back door and yammer for six hours? Or did she just start talking when she saw us in the house through the glass in the door?

The question had a bit of Zen riddle flavor to it because how would I know what she did or didn't do when I wasn't there to hear or not hear her?

Know what I mean?

When Squeeky came in after being outside for a while, she was as predictable as the old village jeweler sucking on his teeth who could never open his doors until he had his first cup of coffee and wound the cuckoo clock.

She'd come in, thank you with a "whirr" sound through pressed lips for FINALLY opening the door, and head straight for the kitchen. Of course, food is a high priority for the wayward. If my belly was mostly empty most of the time, I guess any dining room would be my first stop as well.

Squeeky would chow down on her dry food sounding like somebody walking on gravel, top off her meal with a bunch of slurps at her water bowl, then walk into the middle of the TV room and proceed with her daily ablution: moisten a paw with several good licks and then wipe the sides of her mouth, cheeks, forehead, and what the heck, let's get behind the ears while we're at it.

Who knows what she would have done if she could have held a brush.

When the cleaning job was over, Squeeky would walk over to the sofa and lift her head up to the level of the seat cushions so she could see where the blue shawl was located. When she spotted it, she'd spring up off the floor, do a four-paw landing on that blue shawl, and start her kneading.

Always the kneading. First the kneading. Then decide the nap position. Then take the nap.

While deciding on a nap position, Squeeky performed a walking ritual where she walked slowly in a very tight circle over the immediate area in which she was to lie down and take a snooze. I have no idea why she did that. Someone has told me that other cats do that, too. Maybe most cats. Someone told me that this behavior comes from an ancestral need to walk on and tamp down the weeds and grasses to make a softer bed, which is what wild cats did, and that this need has been passed on genetically through the generations to today's modern cat.

It could be true.

It could also be a simple case of obsessive-compulsive behavior.

Whatever.

Squeeky's nap positions were usually one of two types. Either the classic   on-the-stomach-with-chin-resting-across-front-legs   position   or Squeeky's often preferred "swan dive" pose: as she lay on her side, she'd tuck her chin down to her chest, and extend her front legs straight down her body, almost touching her hind legs.

Her naps were typically three or four hours long.

When Squeeky woke up after a snooze, it was pretty much the same routine as when she came in, except in reverse. Hit the kitchen first, then head for the back door. It became a matter of filling the belly as fuel for the journey, preparing for the road ahead, even if the distance to be covered was the usual 100 feet to the neighbor's and back.

Sun

Squeeky liked a lot of the outside things.

Like long dark green blades of grass. Sweet smelling flowers. Birds who were a little hard of hearing and a touch slow of wing.

But her favorite thing outside may have been the sun.

It wasn't a daytime vs. nighttime issue, because Squeeky, like all cats, was nocturnal. She loved prowling at night.

I think it was the warmth the sun provided.

I think she had spent too much time trying to get warm when the sun wasn't around, and she concluded the sun substitutes she had used, like boxes and bunches of leaves, were minimally effective.

When we'd let her out in the morning, if there was a shadow cast on a portion of the back porch, Squeeky would walk to an area of unobstructed sunlight and sit there. If the entire porch was in shadow, Squeeky would simply go down the back steps and find some spot on the patio that was in sunlight. That's where she'd go and sit and get her bearings, warm her body and bones, check out the lay of the land, see what was coming, what was going, and figure out what she was going to do that day.

She loved sleeping in the sun.

She often slept on the walkway in front of the house. I'd look out the front windows and I'd see her lying there in deep sleep, all stretched out like she was trying to become two cats long.

When her sun-exposed side got a little too warm, she'd give herself a short-order cook's flip and let her other side bake a while.

On really warm days, when she got too hot, she'd go underneath the green hedge that lined our front yard. It was always dark and the dirt was cool, and when she tucked herself into one of the cozy spaces along the bottom, she knew she could sleep there safely and undisturbed, in the yard that had become familiar, next to a house that offered food and water when she wanted it, in which there were a couple of humans who did not chase her away, but instead, were delighted to see her.

Squirrel Dreams

To the uninformed passing eye, our house and yard looks the picture of funky California domesticity. Up front, out by the sidewalk, a curved gate in the middle of a four foot tall hedge opens to a walkway that neatly splits the front yard into two rectangular sections. On one side, a tulip tree sits in the middle, surrounded by a green lawn. The lawn also fills the other side, right up to a medium-sized privit tree located in front of the house. Below the living room windows, facing the street is a long window box, filled with lovely multi-colored flowers.

The tranquil scene is a sham.

With Squeeky's arrival, the front yard and back patio became recurring scenes of face-offs, tense drama, and dark comedy.

Either Squeeky's mother was a good hunter and teacher, or Squeeky, fending for herself in the Edelen Ave. neighborhood, developed hunting skills on her own that allowed her to survive.

Any passing bird momentarily stopping in our yard to pick at the insects in our lawn had a high probability of falling into the sight line of two blue eyes, barely noticeable, staring out of the darkness at the bottom of the hedge. At first, the unblinking eyes are distant, hardly real. Then the eyes move without motion. They seemingly float toward their desired destination, and close in at great speed.

Goodbye, bird.

Squeeky chased squirrels but was never a match for their quickness and agility. A zig-zagged pursuit across the lawn never resulted in a squirrel souvenir for Squeeky. The squirrels were just too fast!

A Short Docudrama

"Squeeky vs. The Squirrel"
Ready?   Set?   Action!

69

SQUEEKY pounces . . . but the SQUIRREL bullets away like it was shot from a squirrel gun . . . then the SQUIRREL leaps into the privit tree, sprints up the trunk, jumps the chasm from tree to rooftop, dashes across the roof, lunges to another tree, and finally hops onto a telephone pole that has a small platform twenty feet up from the ground.

The SQUIRREL is out of breath.

The SQUIRREL sits on the platform and looks down.

SQUEEKY sits at the base of the telephone pole and looks up.

The SQUIRREL barks at Squeeky.

The SQUIRREL is saying, "Screw you, cat."

SQUEEKY, composed and oozing feline patience, talks back to the squirrel, making a guttural chirping sound, saying, *"There'll be another day oh bushy tailed scavenger, and on that day the tree will be just a little bit farther away than you realized. You won't be able to make the tree in one hop. It will take two or three hops. And when you spring for the trunk on that third hop you won't be going anywhere because your tail will be in my tight little fist, and your ASS WILL BE MINE!"*

That was Squeeky's squirrel dream.

But it was only a fantasy that never happened.

Besides, she wouldn't know what to do with a squirrel if she did catch one.

Now lizards were a different matter.

Lizards And Their Legs

Lizards have some disadvantages when they are being pursued.

Based on my personal observations, lizards don't hop real well.

So there goes the now-you-see-me-now-you-don't potential getaway from a pursuer.

Because most lizards drag a tail almost as long as their bodies, I think the extra weight prevents them from generating any speed in a chase scenario.

Another problem for lizards is that their legs don't seem built right for running.

Lizard legs are sort of attached to lizard bodies at right angles, which prevents their legs from being extended forward sufficiently to generate a power stroke and any meaningful speed.

Therefore, when Squeeky went after the lizards it was no contest.

It was like a super star sprinter in the 100 yard dash against a midget with bowed legs.

(No offense intended to the bow-legged midgets out there. You have the same rights as anyone. You can buy ice cream whenever you want and choose any stockbroker you like to lose money for you. Just don't go entering any track meets.)

(No offense intended to the stockbrokers out there.)

Gurple

If a cat likes you, and if the cat is a good hunter, it'll bring its catch to you to show you what a good cat it's been.

Swell.

Squeeky must have loved us. Because if I hadn't periodically removed the bird or lizard or mouse or gopher and whatever that chewed-up dark thing was that Squeeky once brought to the back door, our porch would have been quickly transformed into a wild animal cemetery.

It would have been difficult to open the door without leveling all the tiny tombstones erected in honor of all the former residents of Edelen Ave. who had fallen victim to Squeeky's marauding attacks.

Whenever Squeeky came home after being outside a while she always came to the back door, sat in front of that lower corner window pane, looked in, and started talking – to let us know she was there and would someone please come and open the door and let her in.

Which we always did.

Now, when Squeeky brought her latest catch to the back door, her vocalizations were muffled, because she tried to talk while still holding her catch in her mouth. She sounded a bit like you do when you try to respond to your dentist's question of "Does that hurt at all?" and you have a cotton wad, a drill, a mirror, and the dentist's hand and arm up to his elbow halfway down your throat, and the only answer you can give is "gurple."

If Cindy and I were sitting in the TV room and heard "gurple" at the back door, we knew that Squeeky had reduced the wildlife population of Los Gatos yet one more time.

We also learned that if we heard "gurple" we should not open the back door. To do that would invite Squeeky, and whatever was in her mouth, inside the house.

One time, after hearing Squeeky at the back door, I opened the door while I continued to read a book I had to finish that day because it was due at the library. I didn't pay much attention to Squeeky as she stepped inside, dropped a dead mouse on the floor, then batted it ten feet into the kitchen. Her proud strut saying, *"Here's dinner. Let's eat."*

To prevent this from recurring, we developed the "gurple" response.

Whenever Cindy or I heard "gurple," we'd go to the back door and carefully look at Squeeky. We'd look for either feet or feathers hanging out of Squeeky's mouth, confirming the sound we heard as a "gurple." Then one of us would go out the front door, circle around to the back of the house, and go up the back porch steps, where Squeeky sat facing the door. (We couldn't just slightly crack open the back door to get at Squeeky. All she needed was the tiniest doorway opening, and she'd shoot into the house.) While petting and praising Squeeky for being such a good hunter, we'd entice her into dropping her catch, which we'd then remove with a broom and dustpan.

Squeeky always looked mystified at the dead animal's disappearance. She'd look left, right, walk in a circle, then start talking: *"I could swear that thing was dead. It sure looked dead. I guess it wasn't dead. If it wasn't dead, where did it go? How could it just vanish?"*

The "gurple" response worked well, as long as we accurately identified a "gurple," and did not mistake it for a non-gurple. Confusing the two sounds could lead to a situation, preferably avoidable, like this one:

It happened on a Saturday afternoon in October. I remember that because I had been watching a college football game on TV and I had been wishing for brisk Fall weather like I used to experience growing up in Illinois.

I heard Squeeky at the back door and thought she had muttered normally, asking to be let in. But she hadn't. She had "gurpled."

When I opened the door, just like the time before, I wasn't really paying attention as to whether or not Squeeky had anything in her mouth. I wasn't expecting her to be carrying anything. But she was. Then she dropped what she was carrying right at my feet.

I looked down and saw a six inch lizard.

Which was very much ALIVE!

It was not looking real pleased at having spent some time in a cat's mouth.

The lizard looked angry. He kept opening and closing his lizard mouth at me.

I didn't know what to do.

I wasn't going to pick him up with my bare hands. Ugh.

I ran to get the broom and dustpan.

Squeeky ran after me, yammering, *"Did I do good? Did I? Did I?"*

As I ran back with the broom and dustpan, Squeeky ran alongside me and then sprinted past me, heading for the lizard. We were having fun!

Squeeky got to the lizard before I did and snatched it in her mouth.

"No!" I shouted. I didn't even want to think of what Squeeky might do next.

Then I flashed on what to do! Just pick Squeeky up with the lizard in her mouth and throw them both out of the house!

I grabbed Squeeky, and when I did, I guess I startled her. She quickly turned toward me and said "waark?" But in order to say "waark" and not "gurple," Squeeky needed a mouthful of air. And dropped the lizard.

Who hit the ground running.

That lizard's mama may have raised one ugly boy, but he wasn't stupid. He was a quick learner. He was getting away from that cat's mouth and he was moving those right-angled legs as fast as his long tailed body would let him.

There's a line from an old blues song that goes, "If it wasn't for bad luck I'd have no luck at all." That line was written by that lizard and dedicated to me, because instead of going through the open back door like a good luck lizard, he ran towards the opposing wall, which held an ancient gas wall heater with a slight space beneath it that housed the pilot light and gas lines. Of course, that lizard squeezed into that space under the wall heater and DISAPPEARED INTO THE WALL!

Now that's a BAD LUCK LIZARD!

At the bottom of the wall heater was a small hinged door that opened to permit access to the pilot light. I quickly opened the door and looked for the lizard. I didn't see him. I stuck my face into the small opening to try and get a better look. No lizard. I didn't push my face in too far because I was afraid he might bite my nose. As I was wondering what to do next, Squeeky came over and stuck her head next to mine.

The two of us were looking into the dark recesses underneath the gas wall heater like a couple of coal miners staring into a dark tunnel wondering what was up ahead.

At that moment Cindy came into the room and wanted to know what was going on. What were we doing?

I thought of making up a story because I knew that Cindy would not be overjoyed to hear that a lizard was running loose within our house. I wasn't exactly thrilled with the idea, either. Lizards can climb walls, which probably means they can also make it onto ceilings which means that our lizard could at some point be on our bedroom ceiling. We lived in earthquake country and he was a bad luck lizard. Added up, the possibility, however improbable, was too nasty to contemplate. I had to fess up.

"Squeeky and I are looking for a lizard," I said and told Cindy the whole story.

Then the three of us looked for the lizard. We used a flashlight, a broomstick, and a plastic ruler to poke around that wall heater. I banged on a pot with a wooden spoon. No lizard. Squeeky pressed herself flat on the floor to better see the heater's underside and sniffed all around it. No lizard. I shouted into the metal covering of the wall heater which sounded echoy and loud, "Come on, you! Get out of there!" No lizard.

Squeeky lost interest and went to take a nap on her blue shawl.

Cindy got disgusted with both of us and started watching a cooking show on public television.

It was up to me to rectify the situation.

I left the hinged door at the bottom of the wall heater open and stared at the opening for about five minutes. Then I had an idea. I got a book to read and sat in a kitchen chair which was about eight feet from the heater. I positioned myself in such a way, that as I read the book, the corner of my right eye had an unobstructed sight line to the wall heater. I would have noticed any movement. I had the broom and dustpan ready. When he came out, I thought I could execute a quick capture and transport the lizard outside to his proper environs. But the lizard never showed.

Then Cindy asked a very good question.

"What'll happen when the heat comes on?" she asked

To which I had an honest answer.

"I don't know," I said.

I thought of Cindy's father's philosophy about most situations in life. It seemed applicable now. He had said on more than one occasion, "Either it'll work out, or it won't." He was Irish and came from a family of 11 brothers and sisters that farmed potatoes in Idaho.

After several hours passed without a lizard sighting, we abandoned the hunt. We didn't forget about him, but since he never came out from underneath the wall heater, we hoped he had discovered a way out of the house. We thought he might have found a small opening in the floor and slithered his way into the crawl space below, and escaped to freedom via the foundation cracks and crevices that exist in every old house.

Now that he was gone, we could laugh about that lizard and tell my mother the story of the day Squeeky brought a lizard into the house and we'd say, "That Squeeky! Isn't she something?" My mother would say, "What a pistol. I wonder what she'll bring home next?" And we'd laugh at the humor in this story.

If that had been how it ended.

But it didn't end that way.

It ended later. Two weeks later. Not days. Two WEEKS later.

It was about five or six o'clock one morning when Cindy's scream woke me.

I sat up in bed trying to focus my eyes when Cindy ran into the bedroom and leaped onto the bed and pulled the covers over her head.

"What is it?" I said. "What's going on?"

She poked her arm out from under the covers and pointed towards the bathroom and said, "There."

I looked into the bathroom. The light was on and everything was white. Except for the dark blob in the middle of the bathroom floor. The lizard was back.

I couldn't believe it! It was the same lizard! I also couldn't believe that I could recognize that lizard. But I did! All lizards do not look the same.

Where did he come from?

Had he been inside the house for TWO WHOLE WEEKS?

Or had he gotten out and then decided to come back in?

Why would he want to come back?

It's so much nicer outside.

OMYGOD! What if he has friends and family!

The thought of several lizards scuttering around the floors of our house prompted me to take immediate and decisive action. I leaped from the bed and went to get the broom and dustpan from the hallway closet. To do so I had to step over the lizard. Which I did boldly, determined to protect my family. The lizard appeared perplexed by my giant leg stepping over him. He just followed my movements with quick jerks of his head and blinked his lizard eyes rapidly.

I whooshed him into the dustpan and pinned him there with the broom as I sprinted for the back door. Out on the back porch I thought about letting him go there, but then I thought that was too close to our house and a possible re-entry. So I went over to our neighbor's house, Glen and Muriel's, opened their side gate and crept into their backyard. It was early and still quite dark, so I figured no one would see me, or the dustpan I held with a tail hanging over its side. I set the dustpan on the ground and watched the lizard slither to freedom among a row of flowers.

It then occurred to me that it wasn't that much of a series of lizard wriggles between Glen and Muriel's yard and ours. Fences are not major obstacles for reptiles. Or for cats either, for that matter. Squeeky regularly jumped over that fence and prowled in the yard. What would prevent her from finding the lizard again? If she did find that lizard, I knew she would bring him to the back door again, expecting praise for a hunt well done.

.Before Squeeky entered our lives, when I'd come home from work, I plunked down in my favorite chair and either watched a little TV news or read a book I had checked out of the library. These were simple pleasures I had grown accustomed to enjoy without interruption.

Now that we had Squeeky, life was more challenging. A certain amount of energy was required for constant vigilance. It was quite difficult to give full attention to anything, even casual conversation, when part of you was listening, carefully and preventively.

*   *   *

"Was that one?"

"No."

"How about that?"

"Close, but no."

"Did you hear that?"

"Oh, yeah. Now THAT was a gurple. Is it your turn or mine?"

The Faucet Fixation

Squeeky was happy with her food and water choices until my parents took care of her while we were gone for a week's vacation.

It's not as if my mother introduced Squeeky to stuffed cabbage rolls with Squeeky developing a gourmand's taste for a revolving menu of eclectic entrees. It was not the food at all. It was the water. Let me explain.

In the kitchen, next to the stove, we had placed two bowls for Squeeky. One for food, the other for water. Up to that time, Squeeky had used both bowls just fine. Once in a while, we'd get a new food choice, thinking that Squeeky might like something different, and she'd sniff it, maybe give it a lick or two, then look up at us, say something like "waaa," and walk away.

Cindy and I quickly learned that "waaa," when voiced at mealtime, meant that whatever was in the food bowl was not acceptable at that particular moment. Maybe on another day. Like the day we celebrate the discovery that the earth really is flat after all. But not before that day.

When Squeeky rejected her food, she'd get a disturbed and disjointed look in her face that said she would sooner walk around outside with her mouth open in hopes a bird would fall into it than eat the concoction in her food bowl.

We'd grab another cat food flavor from the cupboard, and if the cat food gods were kind, Squeeky would eat that one. If she didn't like the new flavor, we'd reach for a can of the tried and true: tuna. The stinkier the better.

But water was water. It had never been a problem. Besides, what other options were there? There were no other choices other than water in the water bowl. Until my mother showed up. Then the two of them, Squeeky and my mother, found something better. Forevermore, I mean FOREVERMORE, Squeeky only wanted the better choice and howled like a coyote until she got it.

But I'm not blaming my mother.

It was not her fault that Squeeky seemed so darn cute when she jumped onto the bathroom cabinet and stuck her face right next to my mother's as Mom was finishing brushing her teeth.

Squeeky was curious and Mom was delighted with Squeeky's curiosity and said to her, "Want to try some fresh water, pussy cat?"

My mother turned the cold water on to a slow and steady stream to see what Squeeky would do.

Intrigued by the flow of water, Squeeky stepped into the bathroom sink with her front paws, being careful not to let the water touch her legs or body. She kept her rear end and hind legs on the upper flat portion of the sink, then proceeded to lick at the cold, fresh water.

For Squeeky, that water, right out of the faucet was Manna, The Rainbow's End, and a $100 million dollar lottery ticket wrapped into one liquid jackpot.

Squeeky wouldn't stop drinking from the faucet.

My mother had to grab her and pull her away. She wouldn't stop drinking!

My mother was afraid Squeeky was going to pee all night. And Squeeky was sleeping with my parents in our bed.

When Cindy and I came home from our vacation trip my mother proudly announced that Squeeky had learned something new. We walked in the door and the first thing Mom said was, "You want to see what Squeeky can do?"

*   *   *

Now for the unbelievable but true, goofy yet real, consequences of Squeeky's water-from-the-faucet discovery, Parts A and B.

Part A

Squeeky never drank from her water bowl again.

For 19 years we'd put fresh water in her water bowl every day, and for 19 years Squeeky walked right past it on her way to the bathroom. In the early years she at least looked at the bowl as she walked by. Then, in her mind, the bowl ceased to exist as a viable source of drinkable water. It became more of an ad for what she knew she could get fresher and colder from the faucet in the bathroom, if she hopped up on the sink and hollered loud enough.

Then comes the bizarre, but equally true, Part B.

Part B

Squeeky would happily drink any water she found outside the house.

She'd lap at puddles in the driveway after a rainfall. Watering the lawn produced tiny water pools in the lawn. That, too, was OK. Slurping dirty street water with leaves and scum in it? No problem. But inside the house, usually after eating, or anytime she wanted a drink of water, she always headed for the bathroom sink.

I tried ice cubes in her water bowl, thinking that making it colder might make it more appealing. Nope.

I'd fill the bowl with fresh water and follow her around the house and when she'd stop and look up at me with a "*What are you doing?*" stare, I'd put the water bowl right in front of her. She'd look at the bowl, then back up at me. Her face said, "*Nice try,*" then she'd head for the bathroom sink.

She'd jump up on the sink and look down at the faucet. When glaring at the faucet didn't produce any water, Squeeky would start squawking, yammering, and yowling until one of us turned the water on.

I called a local veterinarian and asked him if a cat could hurt itself by not drinking water, like getting seriously dehydrated. He said, "What do you mean?"

"My cat won't drink from its water bowl," I said.

"How does it get water?" the vet said.

"She waits for us to turn on the faucet in the bathroom," I said. "She only wants to drink water if it's coming right out of the faucet."

"Most cats like fresh water," the vet said.

"But even if I put fresh water in the bowl, even if I make sure the cat sees me putting water in the bowl right from the faucet, she won't drink the water. She'll only drink it if it comes directly out of the faucet into her mouth," I said.

"Your cat apparently has a faucet fixation," the vet said.

"So what do I do?" I said.

"I don't know," the vet said. "I'm not a therapist." And hung up.

*   *   *

We made one final attempt to break Squeeky of her faucet habit. We closed the bathroom door and put Squeeky's water bowl in front of it. I told Cindy that we couldn't open that door until Squeeky drank from her bowl. Squeeky could not see us go into the bathroom. If we had to use the bathroom, we could go down to the library. Librarians are nice people. They would understand.

The moment of truth came when Squeeky had a little snack, then needed to wash it down. She walked over to the bathroom and sat down by the door and howled. Even though she was sitting RIGHT NEXT TO HER BOWL OF WATER!

We sat tight in the TV room and refused to open the door.

Then she howled even louder.

Then she walked into the TV room where we were pretending to read and ripped off a series of screeches and emotional moans. It was her body, but she was possessed by a water demon. We needed an exorcist.

"We can get through this," I said.

Squeeky started racing from room to room, wailing pathetically. She was like a junky going through withdrawal.

"This is crazy," Cindy said.

Squeeky kept wailing and howling and moaning non-stop. Her pupils were dilated. I had never seen an animal so agitated. The whole thing was making us extremely nervous. We tried to hang on. To not give in. I put my hands over my ears to muffle the screeching. It didn't help. This cat had reached decibel levels previously attained only by the civil air defense air raid warning system.

"I can't take it anymore," I said.

"What are you going to do?" Cindy said.

"I'm going to call that vet and tell him he was of no help at all. Then I'm going to call my mother and tell her that she and Dad don't have to take care of Squeeky any more," I said.

But first I went to the bathroom and turned on the faucet.

Fleas

All I know about fleas I learned from Squeeky.

Within the folds of her fur was an encyclopedia of flea knowledge. Not to mention a bunch of fleas.

The first fact I learned about fleas was that they bite.

I already knew fleas caused itching and scratching, but I didn't realize they bit you to get the process started.

When the fleas bit Squeeky she'd jump and run to another room as if the room was the problem. Sometimes she'd jump straight up in the air, all four legs leaving the ground simultaneously. She looked like a pop-up cartoon cat.

The flea collar we had put on her was better at holding her name tag than it was at repelling fleas, so one day I went to the pet store and found out fact number two about fleas. Their irritating behavior had created an entire industry for their elimination.

Pet stores sell flea spray, flea combs, flea powder, flea aerosol bombs, flea shampoo, plastic flea collars, elastic flea collars, even anti-flea medicine you gave your pet that somehow repelled fleas. The pet store salesperson said it was quite popular. I didn't know how this medicine worked. I had visions of Squeeky glowing in the night. I settled for a flea comb.

Flea combs have long teeth that are tightly spaced so when you comb a cat, the fleas get trapped and pulled out of the cat's fur by the tightly spaced teeth.

This was no could-there-be-life-on-other-planets comb. This flea comb actually worked!

The first time I combed Squeeky, I pulled the comb through her fur and when I looked down at the comb I saw two fleas squirming on the teeth of the comb. I squished one of them right on the spot. The other one jumped for his life off the comb onto the carpet right next to where Squeeky was lying down.

83

That's when I learned the third amazing fact about fleas. They can really jump! I looked at how small that flea was and how far he jumped and I calculated it was like a basketball player jumping from one end of the basketball court and dunking the ball at the opposite end!

Nice hops for the fleas.

Despite their leaping abilities and miniscule size which made locating them quite challenging, in the ensuing years I managed to annihilate a large number of fleas that Squeeky had carried into the house.

I never noticed any species variation among the flea population. They all pretty much looked alike: dark with curve shaped bodies looking kind of humpy. They were like a shrunken army of biting hunchbacks.

At that point in time when I realized flea collars didn't work, and the flea combing sessions with the resultant flea massacres making me feel a little ghoulish, I decided to give Squeeky a flea bath, hoping that a good bath with flea shampoo would do the trick.

Cindy said that at one of the local veterinary hospitals they gave flea baths for $25. I said that was a waste of money. We could give Squeeky a bath by ourselves.

Everybody knows cats don't like water, but I figured a speedy bath shouldn't be any worse for a cat than a summer shower in a garden of flowers. You just had to know how to be quick about it.

I told Cindy I'd hold Squeeky in the kitchen sink, and all she had to do was run some water over Squeeky's body, quickly rub some shampoo on her back and under her belly, then run some water to wash off the shampoo and we'd be done. If each step took no more than a minute, the whole flea bath would be done in 3 minutes. I'd towel off Squeeky and we'd have a flea-free cat.

I picked Squeeky up and put her in the sink. No problem.

Squeeky was curiously looking around the sink and at us, and, of course, talking. "Weeek, ska-work, waark," with just a hint of what-are-you-doing-to-me anxiety in her vocal tone.

"Are you ready?" I asked Cindy. "Remember, you gotta work fast."

"I'm ready," Cindy said.

Cindy ran some water over Squeeky and Squeeky flinched and went "Waa-REKK!?!"

As Cindy poured more water over Squeeky, Squeeky began to squirm and wriggle, trying to slide through my hands.

"Enough with the water," I said. "Do the shampoo. She's getting a little hard to hold," I said.

Cindy squirted some shampoo onto Squeeky's back and began working up a lather. That's when Squeeky got real agitated. She began screeching like a smoke alarm and started to struggle in earnest to get out of that sink and out of the clutches of the two sickos trying to drown her.

"Go faster," I hollered at Cindy. "I can't hold Squeeky much longer." Controlling a wiggling wet cat was one thing. But trying to hang on to a riled cat covered in shampoo was like a 50-year-old fat man trying to hang on to his youth. It wasn't gonna happen.

"What happened to the 3 minute bath idea?" Cindy said as she shampooed Squeeky faster and faster.

"That was a bad idea," I said. "A one minute bath is a better idea."

Then Squeeky squirted up through my hands and stuck her face right up against mine. We were nose to nose. I don't know if a cat's eyes can change color, but at that moment I looked into Squeeky's eyes and found no trace of the pretty blue I liked so much. All I saw were two black pools of anger and disgust.

I tried to lower Squeeky back down into the sink, but she extended her front legs onto my chest, grabbing my polo shirt with her paws, and started slithering up towards my left shoulder, struggling to execute a grand leap to freedom from her personal watery hell.

I managed to get a halfway decent hold around her hind legs and was ready to plop her into the sink when Squeeky got a better hold on me. Literally. She had sunk her claws into and through my polo shirt and into my chest.

I don't remember exactly what I hollered, but it was something like: "Yeow, Mama, oh Mama, oh Yeow, Yeow, YEOW!"

I dropped Squeeky on the kitchen floor. She stood there momentarily not knowing what to do. She may have been stunned by her freedom, or warily bracing herself for the next unknown event. She kicked out her left rear leg in an attempt to get rid of some shampooy water. Then she kicked out her right rear leg. Finally, she went to a corner in the kitchen and gave her whole body a shake. It wasn't working. She couldn't get rid of the shampoo. She looked like she had fallen into a white wedding cake.

Cindy went to get a large bath towel to wipe off the shampoo and dry her off.

I took off my polo shirt and looked at the holes Squeeky had carved into the fabric. There were six of them.

I looked down at my chest and saw six matching claw marks, like six tiny bullet holes.

Squeeky sat in the corner, a sad, wet mess looking less angry and a lot more forlorn. She was probably wondering about what had just happened. *"Life had been so good, so easy. Food, blue shawl, wandering around a nice yard, giving dirty looks to an occasional squirrel, and then this water thing came along. Why did they do that to me?"*

I looked at Squeeky, her fur plastered against her skin, and I was amazed at how tiny she was. She looked half her usual size. Without all the fur, cats can be pretty scrawny looking. Squeeky didn't even look like a cat. She looked like an oversized noodle doing an impersonation of a cat.

Watching Cindy towel dry Squeeky I came to two realizations:

First Realization: We were never going to try and give Squeeky a bath again.

Second Realization: I was really beginning to love this cat.

The "Skawerk" Translation

This was the evening program:

After supper, Squeeky would hop up onto her blue shawl and sleep until around 9:00 p.m. Then she'd wake up, have a little snack, and head for the back door, asking to be let outside for a stroll around the house. But sometimes after a bite to eat, Squeeky would go right back to the shawl. What made the difference was the weather outside.

In the wintertime, I'd open the door for Squeeky and the rush of cool, damp air would hit her face and she'd scrunch up her eyes like she was bracing herself for a snowball in the chops. She'd sniff the evening air trying to determine if the mysteries of the dark were worth giving up the comfort of her shawl. She'd stand in the middle of the open doorway, her front legs outside and her hind legs inside, trying to make up her mind.

"So what do you want do?" I'd ask impatiently. "Do you want to go out or are you staying in?"

Often she'd look up at me and say "skawerk" and turn around and go back inside.

They say if you live in a foreign country long enough, you can pick up the language just by hanging with the locals. I know the same phenomenon applies to understanding an animal. After many months of being exposed to Squeeky's considerable vocabulary, I knew what "skawerk" meant.

It's not what she said when she saw a bird or squirrel.

It had nothing to do with food.

A rough, but not inaccurate translation is: "Are you nuts for trying to get me to go outside on a night like this?"

The Whistle Translation

Warm summer evenings were a different matter.

The air seemed softer and sweeter and carried smells whose origin required investigation.

Dark recesses in the backyard were not foreboding like they were in winter. Now they invited exploration.

And off Squeeky would go.

In the summertime, Squeeky's 9:00 o'clock evening walk usually took anywhere between thirty minutes to an hour. If she was having a particularly pleasant evening stroll, she'd dawdle and stretch that hour up to the point where we'd have to call for her to come inside.

One of us would go out on the back porch and call her

"Heeeeeere, Squeeky."

Then wait a little bit.

When she responded to our call, we could hear her rustling through the bushes as she came home, occasionally muttering, probably saying something like, *"Geez, what's the rush? I'm coming. Relax, I'm coming. Hang on to that door for a minute. I'm coming."*

Several times, though, even after we had repeatedly called her, Squeeky did not show up. Either she didn't hear us, or more likely, she simply refused to come.

Imagine that. A cat not coming when it's called.

Once I saw Squeeky through the pickets in Glen and Muriel's fence. I called her and she lifted her head up and looked in my direction. You could almost see the thought balloon appear over her head, carrying the words, *"Should I or shouldn't I?"* Then she turned her head to stare in another direction as the words in the balloon changed to *"Naw. Not just yet."*

Sometimes, as a concession to our efforts to get her inside, after hearing us call she'd take a couple of steps in the direction of our house.

But the seductive powers of the dark outdoors would be too tough to break, and she'd stop her walk home to sit and stare and listen, satisfying her innate cat's curiosity.

We needed something else to get her attention and make her come home. Something she could recognize as the final call before the door got locked and the lights turned off. Something like a whistle.

I created a two tone, high-low whistle, whose intention was to tell Squeeky she had better get back right now if she wanted to spend the night on her shawl indoors rather than outside on a dusty pile of leaves.

Squeeky must have got all that because she usually came a minute or two after I whistled.

I don't know who was more surprised. Me or Cindy.

Squeeky didn't act surprised at all.

What's Mine Is Mine And What's Yours Is Mine

Even with its wondrous powers, the whistle didn't always work. It was not catproof. There were those times when the whistle's transmission was apparently garbled or lost, or a better bet, was ignored by the intended recipient, who over the years had manifested stubborn and willful tendencies.

I would try the whistle once, twice, a few more times, giving Squeeky every opportunity to come in for the night. But if several minutes passed without us seeing her trotting up those back steps or anywhere in the back yard, we'd close and lock the door, turn off the lights, and go to bed.

Squeeky would spend the night outside.

We now know that was bad cat management. But Cindy and I were young and untrained as cat parents. We didn't know, as we found out in time, that things can happen out there in the corners of the night. Squeeky could have run into a gang of raccoons, or possums with an attitude, or a tow truck driver driving hell-bent with a repossessed BMW, or encountered vicious chickens. Or the worst possibility of all, have met another cat.

What we discovered, courtesy of Squeeky and her cohorts, is that cats are extremely territorial.

I never knew that.

I know that now.

If Native Americans had had a few cats around, they never would have given up the island of Manhattan. The cats wouldn't have let them.

Within each cat's brain there exists a mythical set of boundary lines which defines the geographical territory in which they reside and into which no other cat must be allowed to enter. Any cat trespassing, intentionally or unintentionally, into another cat's territory is subject to First: receiving an evil stare, Second: being slowly stalked with a menacing stroll, <u>Third</u>: hearing the Banshee Cat Scream from a mouth wide open and about six inches away.

If none of these actions causes the transgressing cat to leave the territory into which it has ventured, then option number <u>Four</u>, a fang-baring, claws-slashing, ass-whipping will follow.

All this turmoil because cats are selfish about the patch they call home.

What the heck's the matter with 'em?

As much as cats value the territory that they have proclaimed their own and will defend up to and including the ass-whipping stage, they think nothing of walking into another cat's territory, and checking out the flora and fauna! Where's the respect for that which belongs to another? Why can't they be satisfied with their own yards?

WHAT THE HECK'S THE MATTER WITH 'EM?

Squeeky proved to be extremely territorial. Nothing else on four legs was allowed into our yard. Whenever that event took place, a scream would pierce the air so powerful and other-worldly, you didn't know whether to grab a gun or a crucifix for protection.

Squeeky was not only a talker.

She also screamed real well.

A Beautiful Buzzing

One night, nothing much was on TV, and both Cindy and I had read books for a couple of hours. Cindy was yawning and I had started to nod off. Every time I woke up I re-read a paragraph I had read earlier and I still didn't know what was going on in the story. We decided to go to bed.

Squeeky had elected to pass on her evening amble and was contentedly sleeping on the sofa on her blue shawl. She was lying on her side, eyes shut tight and breathing slowly. I watched her stomach gently swell and contract with each breathing cycle. It brought to mind the image of a small boat bobbing on ocean swells on a peaceful moonlit night.

Watching Squeeky sleep made me jealous. When she slept she looked as if she had entered a land of no income tax worries, where eating three doughnuts a day was an important part of a healthy diet. Smoking was encouraged.

As we left the TV room to go to the bedroom we both said "Goodnight, Squeeky. See you in the morning."

Squeeky lifted her head up at the sound of our voices. Her eyes, barely opened and unfocused, followed us as we walked out of the room.

By the time I had unlaced my shoes and taken off my jeans that always seemed about ten pounds heavier in the evening than they were in the morning, Cindy had already turned the bed down and jumped in.

I sat down on the bed, and as I reached over to turn off the light, I looked into the bathroom doorway and saw Squeeky sitting there.

She just sat there, not saying anything, which was unusual for her, and looked at us.

She had been in the bedroom before, but not for any length of time. She had always been passing through, either on her way to the front door to be let outside, or on her way to the back part of the house, the TV room, after having spent some time outside.

"Whatchya want, Squeeks?" I said. "You got your shawl, food's in the kitchen, fresh water's there even if you won't touch it, but it's there just in case. It's too late to go outside now. Go back to sleep."

As I reached for the light switch I looked down at Squeeky. Her eyes could have been borrowed from the explorer Ferdinand Magellan. They glistened with discovery and excitement. "Ah, ha!" Squeeky's Magellan eyes said, "So this is where you go at night!"

Still in bed, I propped myself up on my elbows and looked at Squeeky. "Well, now what?" I said.

Squeeky still sat there. Studying the situation.

I got out of bed, bent down and picked her up. I started to take her back to her shawl on the sofa in the TV room, when I had the thought that maybe Squeeky would like to see what it was like on top of the bed. I placed her in the middle of the bed.

At that point, Cindy, who had almost fallen asleep, looked over at Squeeky as she was walking around the top of the bed, going up to each corner, checking out the lay of the land. Making sure there were no trap doors anywhere.

"Hey, Squeeky. Come over here," Cindy said, patting the bedcover by her left side.

Squeeky looked at her and went "werk?" and continued walking around, sniffing the top of the bed.

I went back to the TV room and got Squeeky's shawl and laid it down next to Cindy on the bed.

Squeeky came over immediately and laid down on it.

I turned the lights off as Cindy put her left arm around Squeeky. Squeeky started purring. It was a deep and rhythmic purr that got louder with each passing minute.

The three of us fell asleep in the darkened room, as it filled with the sound of Squeeky's purring, a beautiful soft buzzing sound, that rose and fell, and rose and fell, and rose and fell. Like a chorus of humming butterflies.

The Next Night And 6,435 More

The next night, Cindy was watching an old movie on TV when I padded off to the bedroom with a couple of magazines.

I walked into the bedroom, turned on the light, and found Squeeky in the middle of the bed. She was sitting up, not lying down, and facing the doorway.

I wondered what she was doing.

So I asked her. "What are ya doing, Squeeky?" Squeeky stared at me with open, round eyes as if I were the Ten Commandments and was there to change her life.

As I turned down the bedcovers and slid into bed, Squeeky came up on my left side and lay down beside me, close enough so that I could pet her while I was reading. Then I realized what Squeeky had been doing on the bed when I walked in. She had been patiently waiting for someone to join her. After all, it was bedtime, and this is where we all sleep now, isn't it?

That was the thing about Squeeky.

She was a fast learner and she knew what she liked.

From that first night on, except for those times when we were away on vacation, or visiting someone overnight, Squeeky always slept with us.

She liked to sleep with her backside pressed up against something, like a leg or a back. On chilly winter nights she liked to curl up within an arm that encircled her, or if it was really cold, she burrowed underneath the bedcovers.

Several times, when we stayed up late, Squeeky would come into the TV room, where we usually were, and sit in the middle of the room. She'd try to keep her eyes open, blinking to stay awake, but the weight of a long day sat on her eyelids, and eventually pushed her eyes closed. Squeeky would sit in silence, breathing slowly, dozing, looking like she might topple over at any moment. At first, we couldn't figure out what she was doing, sitting in the middle of the TV room, half asleep. Why didn't she just hop up on her shawl, which we always returned to the sofa, even if we had placed it, for Squeeky, on our bed the night before?

Then, one time when I got up to go to the bathroom, Squeeky immediately opened her eyes and started walking beside me. Which is when we figured out what Squeeky wanted. She wanted somebody to crawl into bed with her.

It got to the point that Squeeky wouldn't really sleep well unless the three of us, the whole family unit, were in bed together. Maybe it was a security thing. The clan bundling together against the unseen elements of the night.

Maybe it provided warmth. Leaning up against each other.

A psychological comfort.

Sense of belonging.

Maybe she just liked being with us.

Maybe it was all of the above.

Likes And Dislikes

Squeeky didn't much like being held.

She liked being petted. That was OK with her. But she had to be on the ground, preferably lying on her side, when you petted her.

If you picked her up and sat down on a chair with the expectation of her staying in your lap you would be disappointed. As soon as you sat down she looked for and took the nearest exit. Up and over a knee, or a quick leap over a leg and she was gone.

She liked being scratched under her chin.

That's a hard to reach area for most cats, so if a cat likes you, you can stick your fingers in there and scratch around a little bit. Squeeky liked that under the chin business. It must have felt good.

Squeeky didn't like you messing with her feet, like holding her by one of her paws, or massaging the soft pink pads under the paws. She wanted those parts left alone.

She did not like "rough rubbing," the way some people dig into a dog's fur with their fingers. It's a quick back-and-forth hand motion with curved fingers usually accompanied by the person saying "Atta, boy."

I don't know why some people try to treat cats as they would a dog. Squeeky would have none of it. If you rough-housed with Squeeky she would shriek, then walk away. If she REALLY didn't like it, she would bite you. That usually got the point across.

Squeeky never liked rock music. It was either the throbbing drum beat or the fact that we liked to turn up the volume on our favorite songs that always caused Squeeky to head for the door to be let out. She didn't mind classical music, though. In fact, I think she enjoyed it. Whenever Cindy would play some of her favorites, Squeeky stayed curled up and continued napping. Maybe the soft strings of gentler classical pieces were soothing to Squeeky, unlike the pounding rhythms of rock 'n roll. She didn't even like the Beatles. I was always a little disappointed in that.

The Time Thing

I wish someone would explain to me the slippery nature of time.
How it can vanish even as you occupy it.
Ponds don't do that.
No road I have ridden or forest trail I have ever walked upon has disappeared while I was still on it.
Time is the ultimate magic act.
It makes things begin to disappear even while they're appearing.
Sometimes time seems to move so slowly as to seem unmoving.
Other times, large chunks of it, like weeks or months, even years move past with alarming speed.

But the real legerdemain, the stuff that bends believability, is the slow and steady trickle of seconds, falling off each day, like beads sliding off a necklace. Until one day, the necklace, and all the pretty beads, are gone.

Things that exist within the context of time can fade so completely, it can seem like they were never around in the first place.

The mysterious movement and magic of time raises several questions, but the most basic question is, "Where does it go?"

The Reason I Bring Up The Time Thing

One day, I was sweeping the driveway, and I momentarily paused and looked at our house and yard. For no particular reason. Sometimes you stop what you're doing and give things a farmer-surveying-his-lower-40 glance.

I noticed the tree in front of the house was getting taller and thicker with leaves. The house looked good but would need a paint job one of these days. Up on the roof, sitting in the middle, at the highest point possible, was Squeeky.

She looked like a weathervane ready to rotate in whichever way the next gust of wind would blow.

Squeeky loved being up on the roof. There was a Bay tree next to the house, and Squeeky could climb up that thing like a squirrel. She'd hug that tree trunk with her front paws, dig in with her claws, then shinny and pump herself up the side of the tree with her strong hind legs. She'd walk out on a good-sized limb that came close to the house, and from there, jump to the roof.

The roof was Squeeky's equalizer. Up there she enjoyed parity with the squirrels. For the birds, I half expected her to leap from the roof, furiously flapping her front paws, in a grand attempt to master the ability to fly. Then those winged suckers would REALLY be in for it!

I thought about the time thing when I realized Squeeky had been with us for 10 years.

Or was it 12?

It seemed like it had been a couple of months.

Changes

During the time Squeeky had been with us, I had come to realize that cats have some amazing physical attributes.

Their vision is excellent.

When Squeeky was in a mellow mood, her eyes, normally almond-shaped, closed into two barely open slits. But they were open enough to take in your hand movements, the door behind you, each and every window in the room, even register a shadow's flickering on a far wall.

Intrigued by a motion or scene that prompted her interest, Squeeky would pop her eyes into two intense circles, yielding a vision so sharp that she'd see things way before the things knew they were being seen or thought they could be seen.

For extra visual power, Squeeky would stare with a concentrated focus on her subject, then she'd push her head forward about half an inch, never blinking, never looking away. That extra half inch must have been the ticket for bringing things up good and close.

A cat's sense of smell is several times more powerful than a human's. It's almost as if their tiny noses were magnetized and attracted any aromatic particles passing by in the air, particles that the human nose did not know even existed.

When it comes to hearing noises from way over there, or sounds you would think were inaudible, cats' hearing abilities make us humans look like we've got rocks for ears.

Once I was lying on the bed listening to a radio talk show. The windows were open. Squeeky was lying next to me on her blue shawl, sound asleep, motionless, deep breathing, when WHAM! She lifted her head up, adjusted her ears like two antennae receiving signals from outer space, then dashed to the window to check out something she had heard. I had heard nothing. I went to the window to see what was going on outside. Didn't see a thing. No fallen tree limb. No burglar tip-toeing by the side of the house with our TV set on his back.

I looked at Squeeky who was motionless and staring down at the ground. I followed her line of sight to a medium-sized rock. On the rock was a medium-sized lizard. The lizard stood motionless on the rock with one of his front legs raised in the air. He knew the jig was up. His previous movement on that rock, though completely silent to me, was like kicking a can of marbles to Squeeky, whose nose and whiskers were pushed up against the window screen, waiting for that lizard to make the next move.

I watched that lizard hold his leg up in the air until I got bored and went back to my book. I think he was determined to stay frozen in space until the sun went down or Squeeky's face disappeared from the window screen, whichever came first.

That's why it was somewhat surprising, when one day I went into the kitchen and saw Squeeky sitting in the middle of the kitchen floor, facing the living room, not seeing me, and I said "Hey, Squeeky" as I often did when I first saw her in the morning, and Squeeky didn't say anything or turn to look at me.

So I said it again, to her backside, "Hey, Squeeky!"

Nothing. No reaction.

I reached out to pet her. I thought maybe she was sick or something. When I touched her she jumped like I'd poked her with a stick and she shrieked "Waa-WAA!"

When I walked into the kitchen, Squeeky had her back toward me. She hadn't seen me. That was understandable.

But she never heard me, either.

Squeeky had gone deaf.

Doc Jen & The Cat Janitor

Then again, maybe she just didn't hear me, I thought.

Maybe she was choosing to ignore me.

Maybe she was simply being stubborn. She didn't come every time she was called, refused to drink from her water bowl, sometimes ate her food voraciously, other times sniffed at her bowl, then would stick her nose up and wander away with a walk that said, "*I'll be on my shawl on the bed. Come get me when you have something serious to offer.*"

That could have been it.

So I got up close, two or three feet away and clapped my hands and again said, "Hey, Squeeky!"

Squeeky just stared straight ahead like she was waiting for a bus.

I told Cindy about it and she took Squeeky to the Los Gatos Dog and Cat Hospital where Cindy had gotten a part-time job as a Cat Janitor.

What else would you call a job where you cleaned up cat litter boxes, played with the kittens and puppies, fed the animals, played some more, watered the plants, played some more. (There was a lot of that playing around going on in the back room.)

Cindy asked one of the doctors, Doc Jennifer, to take a look at Squeeky.

"We think she's losing her hearing," Cindy said.

Doc Jennifer looked in one ear and then the other and said, "Her ear canals are all dark and gooey. Let's clean out her ears, then we'll see what we have."

Doc Jennifer put some drops in her ears to soften up the crud and then gently scooped out a lot of brownish-blackish stuff that might have been the problem.

Cindy brought Squeeky home and described how they had cleaned out Squeeky's ears.

"I bet that was it," I said. "I bet her ears were just clogged up. No wonder she couldn't hear."

We were in the kitchen. Squeeky had gone to her bowl and had something to eat. When she finished she got up and went to the doorway that separates the living room from the kitchen and gave herself a face-cleaning. Her back was to us. I thought I'd try her ears again.

"Hey, Squeeky," I said. Not so loud as to startle her, but loud enough to qualify as a hearing test.

Squeeky finished cleaning her face, then started to walk away.

"Hey, Squeeky," I said again, only a little louder, with a little more hope.

She walked through the living room and hopped on the bed for an early evening nap.

She never turned around once.

Never heard me.

Lester's Orchard

It's the funny how the mind works.

Thinking about Squeeky going deaf made me think of Stan Lester's father's orchard.

Back in the 1960s, when I was in high school and just starting to drive, I used to love driving past an orchard that belonged to the Lester family, whose son was a fellow classmate. This was in the Santa Clara Valley, an area once world renowned for its apricot, cherry, and plum trees, long before it became known as Silicon Valley, birthplace some would say, of the high tech industry: silicon chips and widget makers and designers of things electronic.

Back then, in spring, the trees in Lester's orchard were full of blossoms.

During summer, as the various fruit varieties ripened, the branches bulged with fruit bunches of reds and yellows and purples.

When fall arrived, the fruit had long been picked and sent to canneries in San Jose, and the leaves started to fall and gather between the rows of trees.

In winter the bare tree limbs looked like the hands and arms of poets lifting into the sky.

One day I drove by the orchard and half the trees had been yanked out of the ground and left to lie on their sides. Days later, I came by and saw dozens of large mounds of still smoking ash, all that was left of the trees that had been yanked out of the ground and burned. The rest of the orchard was soon to follow.

Within a year, what had once been a lovely fruit orchard became a development of new homes.

See, people who came to the valley to work for the widget makers and electronic designers needed places to live, and Mr. Lester, without much difficulty, had calculated that his land, if sold to a home builder, could bring in more money in one financial transaction than an orchard full of fruit could produce in many years.

So he did. Sell the land, that is.

It made me very sad when I realized that I would never see those trees again. It was nobody's fault. It was an early lesson that things just don't stay the same forever, even if you want them to.

I remembered that now.

Shouts And Whispers

If you're a cat and can't hear any more, you can't hear a car's engine as it roars closer, or tires whooshing up the road, or the clinking of a dog's name tag against the collar buckle as the dog runs up the sidewalk.

You can't hear footsteps.

Shouts.

Or the whispers of flapping wings as they pass overhead.

Things get a little dicey.

I think Squeeky realized this because she was no longer in such a hurry to leave our yard and go exploring. Now, when we opened a door to let her outside – because she still insisted on going outside every day – she didn't burst through the open doorway and charge outside like she did in her younger years. First she'd stand across the threshold and think things through.

"OK. Take your time. No need to rush.. Look left into the ivy. Survey the whole yard. Peer into the dark area at the bottom of the green hedge. Look right to the car in the driveway, check underneath. Nobody hiding there. Nobody's around. Good."

Then Squeeky would slowly walk outside and go up to the front gate and peek in between the slats to see what was going on out in the street. See if those dogs had gotten out again.

Squeeky was more cautious, but she still wanted to roam. Which seemed too risky, too dangerous without the ability to hear. So Cindy and I agreed that whenever Squeeky was let outside, one of us would go with her. To be her ears and to limit her wandering ways.

When Squeeky started to cross the street, we'd pick her up, bring her back to the middle of the yard, put her down and say "No." Followed by "Stay." As if giving verbal instructions to a deaf cat made sense.

Animals are intuitive, however, and if you say "No" with enough steam and certitude, even if they can't hear the command, they seem to get the idea.

Squeeky did. She stayed put. Sort of. As long as someone was outside, so she could see that person watching her watch the person. You could break eye contact for a while. That was fine. But if you went inside for a drink of water, when you'd come back out, you'd have to go looking for a deaf cat.

Broken Whistle

I wondered what it looked like to Squeeky.

Me standing at the front door saying "Hey, Squeeky, you wanna go out?"

It occurred to me that nobody had told Squeeky that she had gone deaf.

Maybe she thought the world, including me, had lost its voice. In this new world, the front and back doors now closed as if made of cotton, neighborhood cats were seen but not heard, birds hopped and flew in a tuneless void. So Squeeky looked at me quizzically, perhaps in amusement, as my foolish lips moved, but made no sound.

Recognition of physical symbols, however, can serve in place of a previously familiar verbal interchange.

My hand moving toward the door was enough. As soon as Squeeky saw me reaching for the door knob, she slowly walked towards the door. Patiently, she waited for the door to fully open, then in halting steps, as if to steady herself, she walked down the front steps and out on the walkway. She went about fifteen feet, then turned around and looked at me, the look saying, *"Well, are you coming or what?"*

Her look referred to what had become a late afternoon pattern: Squeeky going outside with either Cindy or me.

As I said earlier, Cindy and I weren't comfortable with letting Squeeky roam on her own, so one of us always went out with her.

We had placed one of the back yard patio chairs in the front yard so either one of us could sit and watch Squeeky wherever she chose to lay for her outdoor afternoon catnap.

On my watch, I'd sit in the chair with a book or newspaper, sometimes smoke a cigar, and Squeeky would lie in front of me. If it was a warm day, Squeeky, loving the warmth of the sun, would lie on the cement walkway until she got too hot, then she'd head for some shade. She'd go to either the tulip tree in the left side of the yard which cast a cooling circular shadow, or a closer choice, the area right under the chair.

When it was time to go in, I'd go open the front door, and if Squeeky was awake and watching me, I'd wave my hand with a "come here" motion. She knew what that meant. Sometimes she'd come. Of course, if she was asleep, she literally could not see my hand signal. Then I'd have to pick her up and bring her in. Because the high-lo whistle didn't work anymore.

6 Lessons From A Deaf Cat

So you can't hear. So what? Big deal.

Lesson #1. Walk slower and look around more to see what's going on.

Lesson #2. Once in a while, stop and look all the way around. Check your backside. You never know.

Lesson #3. You don't have to listen to those damn dogs barking from across the street anymore.

Lesson #4. The refrigerator door now opens silently. The tinkle of glass against glass and the rustle of bags being opened no longer tip you to the possibility of mooching snacks. So nap in the living room chair that faces the kitchen. It has an unobstructed view of the refrigerator.

Lesson #5. You lose something, you adjust. It's that simple.

Lesson #6. Remember, you are not loved less. You don't have to love less.

Like Kate Hepburn

Old age and silence arrived about the same time for Squeeky, and she accepted both gracefully, like a movie star accepting an Oscar award with wrinkled hands.

The bustle of her youth had long dissolved into the measured pace and outlook of one who had already been there, had seen it before, and was not going to be impressed by the repetitious or mundane.

Squeeky slept more, ate less, and let one day turn into the next with a measured calm, leaving the adventures of the street to those more willing and foolish, and ultimately, more capable.

She became a picky eater. Fussy and choosy. Once, many years ago when she first came up the back steps of our house, she would eat anything you'd put in a bowl.

Now, her teeth ground down to tiny nubs, chewing dry cat food was difficult, so she preferred moist food. And fresh, please. "*Yes, I'd like a new can. Forget those three partially opened cans in the refrigerator. They're not fresh. And no tuna today. I had tuna yesterday. Today I'd like the crab and shrimp catch, please, but not the whole can. That's way too much. But I would like a few bites of the crab and shrimp catch. I haven't had that recently.*"

In appearance, Squeeky still looked the same.

That's the nice thing about having a lot of fur and hair all over your body. That stuff covers all the wrinkles.

Squeeky's tan coat with the white splotches, milk chocolate streaks, and dark brown markings never changed.

One thing, for sure, didn't change.

When she wanted to, Squeeky still talked as much as the first day I saw her.

With one exception.

Now she talked much louder.

It started when she went deaf. Because she either couldn't hear herself or heard herself very poorly, she must have thought that nobody else could hear her either. So she started talking louder.

What used to be a simple "wawow?" asking to be let out, was now "waWOW?"

Then, "waWOW, waWOW?"

Finally, "WAAWOW!?!"

Like you couldn't hear the first one.

Ah, Those Were The Days

Within the outdoor domain that Squeeky once ruled, she no longer seemed to be the image of terror for birds and squirrels and lizards. Somehow they knew.

Word had gotten out. "Squeeky's slowing down."

Earlier, in her younger years, when we let Squeeky outside and she boldly dashed down the front steps, her body language served notice to all creatures within viewing distance that this was her territory, and if they chose to stay within it, they did so at great risk to their longevity on the planet.

Now, as Squeeky stepped onto the lawn, a bird would look up, see Squeeky, then go back to pecking for bugs, as if to say, "Yeah, yeah, in a minute. I'm almost done here."

Squeeky gave squirrels little more than a cursory glance as they occasionally hopped close to her, daring her with a sarcastic cackle, "Come on, one more sprint down the driveway, for old time's sake."

Once I watched Squeeky as she walked around to the side of the house and down to the Bay tree she used to regularly climb. I remember her climbing that tree with amazing speed, then leaping from the tree to either John's (our neighbor) second story deck, or to our roof. Either location gave her an unparalleled view of her world. Many were the days when Squeeky curled up in a pile of leaves on our roof and spent the afternoon there.

Now she stood at the base of the tree and looked upward. She didn't try to climb it. She knew she couldn't. Didn't have the leg strength or the agility anymore.

I never saw her try to climb that tree and not make it. I wondered if there had been a day when she tried to go up that tree, got up only part of the way, and then, realizing she couldn't make it, jump back down. Or was there a day when she walked up to that tree and simply knew her climbing days were over?

Squeeky looked upward, up at a point where the trunk separated in a v-shape, for the longest time.

Then she walked back to the front yard to take a nap.

Thwump

A wiser point of view often accompanies those who advance into their senior years. But seniors have their own problems.

Squeeky no longer chased what she couldn't catch, and long ago stopped being amused by fake robber rodents. Life now contained fewer mysteries for those who have stuck their nose through the old mouse hole too many times to count.

Squeeky's physical skills, her speed and strength and feline agility, were not what they once were. Which was not a problem. Until Squeeky tried to do what she no longer could do. Then it became a problem.

During all these years (what were we up to now, 13, 14, 15 years?), Squeeky must have used her powerful hind legs at least a million times to hop onto and then over the front gate, onto our car's hood, into an open car window, halfway up a tree chasing a squirrel, every night onto our bed, up on my desktop, and onto the bathroom sink countertop, once, twice, three times a day, ready to ask for some fresh water.

But on her million and first try to jump high, to spring onto the bathroom sink, Squeeky couldn't make it.

I heard the "thwump."

It was preceded by a hectic, frenetic, scrambling series of sounds. Like an ice-skater who's lost his footing and is flailing with his skates trying to regain his balance. Or like a cat trying to hang onto a slick glazed bathroom counter-top with its front paws, as it slowly slides backwards towards the floor below.

Then comes the "thwump."

I walked into the bathroom and I saw Squeeky sitting on the floor, looking up at the bathroom sink.

When she saw me she immediately stood up on all four feet, looked at me, then looked at the bathroom faucet and started talking, "mmreek, mmraa, raarow?"

As I picked Squeeky up, put her in the sink, and turned the water on, I said "You know, we're not around every time you want a drink of water from the bathroom faucet. Now that you can't make it up here on your own, you might consider using your water bowl."

Even as I said these words, I wondered why I bothered saying them.

I knew the water bowl was never going to be an option. Inside the house, water, in order to be consumed by Squeeky, had to come from the bathroom faucet directly to her lips without touching a container.

Later that day Squeeky wanted another drink.

She walked up to the bathroom cabinet and sat there and howled. She wanted to be lifted onto the sink.

I thought this was pushing it.

Whose house was this anyway? Squeeky's or ours?

Who was in charge around here. Squeeky or us?

The three of us knew the answers to both questions and it wasn't even debatable. Squeeky, of course.

But I had an idea.

We had a wooden stool that seemed to periodically move throughout the house, sometimes resting in a corner by itself as an object d'art, sometimes finding a space on the floor alongside a wall, where it did a nice job of holding a large pot of flowers or a framed picture. Sometimes we even used it as a stool.

I put it next to the bathroom cabinet and wondered if this would work. Would Squeeky use the stool as a first step to shorten her leap onto the sink? The way she viewed her water bowl, she might consider the stool a pleasant piece of sculpture, something to sit under while she howled for someone to come pick her up.

Squeeky looked at the stool, then looked up at the bathroom sink. She waited a couple of seconds, perhaps mentally measuring the distance from the stool to the sink, perhaps wondering if she could make this new double jump.

She walked up to the stool and in quick successive leaps went from the floor onto the stool, then onto the bathroom sink, ready for a drink of water.

Who says you can't teach an old cat a new trick?

Or was I the one being taught?

I got another small stool and put it next to the bed.

White Coat Blues

During all this time, Squeeky had never gotten seriously sick, so we never had to see a veterinarian that often. Just periodically, for regular shots and checkups to make sure all of her parts were running OK. Which was a good thing, because Squeeky liked going to the animal hospital about as much as I liked going to the doctor's office.

And I never went.

Unless it was an emergency.

Once, I had a ruptured appendix, only I didn't know it was a ruptured appendix and neither did the doctors. We haggled for a week over the appropriate medical treatment I should receive, while I lay in a hospital bed with a swollen and hurting belly, watching TV.

"We recommend exploratory surgery," the doctor said.

"In your dreams," I said.

"Otherwise there's no way of telling what's wrong with you."

"No. Get away from me."

The Next Day.

"Have you changed your mind?"

"You're standing in front of the TV. Do you mind?"

The Next Day.

"Here's the second opinion you requested. The doctor concurs."

"You must be related. Are you guys related?"

And so on. For a week.

Until one night, I was in a lot of pain, and a janitor came down the hallway, stuck his head in my room and said, "It's probably your appendix. Lose the damn thing."

He was right.

But I still don't like doctors.

Neither did Squeeky.

116

Whenever we took her to the Los Gatos Dog and Cat Hospital, even as we placed her in the car, before we started driving, Squeeky hollered and yelped and wailed. But then, we never took Squeeky in the car to any place but the hospital, and that's where she got poked and prodded, so wouldn't you scream when you got put in a car if you knew what was going to happen to you at the end of the ride?

At one time I thought I might try to train Squeeky not to fear the inevitable consequence of a car ride by taking her around the block once a week, maybe cruise down the main street of downtown Los Gatos, just a short trip, then come home where I'd give her some nice moist tuna parts, fresh out of the can. Give her something positive to look forward to at the end of the car ride. Basic behavioral conditioning.

But I never did.

I decided it wasn't worth going through all the stress and turmoil for any of us, just to try and get Squeeky to calm down for a quick car trip she only had to take about once a year.

Still, as infrequently as we went to the hospital, whenever we had to go, I always wished I had taken the time to try and make Squeeky more amenable to riding in the car. Because as long as we were in the car, Squeeky's siren-like wailing made the five minute trip seem like three hours.

Now it was time to take that car ride once again.

Not because Squeeky needed a shot.

But because she had begun to act a little strange and we didn't know what was going on with her. We thought the folks in the white coats should have a look at her.

117

Say "Waaah"

"So tell me again," the young female veterinarian with a cheerful smile asked, "Why, exactly, am I seeing Squeeky today?"

We were in one of the exam rooms. The veterinarian, Cindy, and I stood around one of the examining tables. Squeeky sat in the middle of the table, not talking all that much. Talking would have drawn attention from the person in the white coat with a stethoscope around her neck, and that's not a good thing to do when you're trying to be invisible.

"She's been acting strangely lately," Cindy said.

"She hasn't been sleeping well. She sleeps a little, maybe half an hour, then she gets up and walks around the house, not as if she wants to go out, more like she's just wandering, not knowing what she wants to do.

"Sometimes she stops at her food bowl and eats a little bit, but I can tell she's not really hungry.

"Then she gets these tiny bursts of energy and she gets real animated. She'll quickly jump on and off the furniture, run around the house, then just as quickly she'll stop running around and start meowing."

I added my own anecdote of Squeeky's recent behaviors.

"One day, when I let her out the back door, she didn't casually sniff the air and check out the backyard like she usually does when she first goes outside. Instead, she sprinted down the back steps and ran over to the neighbor's backyard. Then she sat down on their patio and looked back at me standing at our back door. It was really odd. She seemed confused. Like she wanted to run someplace but didn't know where to run to."

While Cindy and I provided this information, the veterinarian petted and soothed Squeeky, examined Squeeky's ears, gently pried open her mouth to check out her teeth, gums, and tongue, felt all around her neck area, then, with one hand stroked and pressed Squeeky's stomach.

Squeeky made a sound like "waaah."

"Has Squeeky been eating all right?" the veterinarian asked. "She seems a little light to me."

"She's been eating OK," Cindy said. "I haven't noticed any changes there."

"We'll check her weight and compare it to her previous visit," the veterinarian said. "Then we'll give her a complete physical. We'll take a blood sample, do the analysis, and see what turns up."

As the veterinarian started to go to work on Squeeky, Cindy and I walked back into the lobby. Cindy pretended to be unconcerned and looked at a brochure on how to prevent your cat from getting hairballs. I sat down in a black vinyl chair that didn't feel right. It didn't feel like I could sit in it for any length of time. It was a chair that made me want to stand up and start pacing as soon as I sat down in it. Now, what kind of chair is that?

The Ride Home

The ride home from the animal hospital was like a walk in a subway tunnel when the subway workers are on strike. Kinda quiet.

In the past, Squeeky never chattered on the way back from the hospital. This time was no different. She sat in Cindy's lap in the passenger seat and silently watched the houses flip past the window. I always thought she looked a little indignant during the ride home, outraged that she had been abused by the people in the white coats, and betrayed by the two of us.

As we got closer to home, Squeeky became a bit less sullen. She put her front paws on the dashboard and looked straight ahead. Then she left Cindy and came over to my side, sat in my lap, and looked out the driver's side window.

We made the left turn at the fire house and Squeeky perked up a little more and muttered something barely audible.

The usual right turn down Edelen Ave. took us toward our house, and Squeeky started squirming as she recognized the neighborhood and anticipated the end of the car ride. Home was near.

We pulled into the driveway and Squeeky could hardly wait to get out of the car.

As the three of us went inside our house, Squeeky headed right for her food bowl. Arriving home safely after a visit with the white-coated people always justified a celebratory meal.

Cindy went outside to work in the garden.

I sat down to watch TV.

We both wondered what the veterinarian was going to say.

A Veterinarian's Life, A Biographical Sketch

The young girl, while walking on her way to school, observes a squashed frog by the side of the road. She remembers that frog for later.

On her way home from school the young girl walks with a rapid pace. She hurriedly passes Hillman's Grocery Store, not stopping as she often does, to say hello to Mrs. Hillman, a friend of her mother's. Walking down Scott St. she passes a very large oak tree. As soon as she passes the tree, she makes an immediate left turn and walks over to the street curb and looks down into the gutter. It is still there. Non-squeamishly, she picks up the squashed frog and slips it into a zippered compartment of her backpack. She takes it home and attempts to revive the frog.

It does not work. The frog stays squashed.

One summer, this same young girl observes a bird hopping around the yard on one leg. The other leg is bent at an angle that is not normal. The girl walks up to the bird, reaches down, and grabs the bird before it can fly away. As she holds the bird in her right hand, she reaches out with her left hand and touches the bend in the bent leg, and says, "Poor little bird." The bird does not appear to be in any pain. But the girl wonders: How would anybody but the bird know if it is in pain? Then she opens her right hand. The bird flies away.

Many years later, the girl is at work.

She picks up the phone and dials a number. She listens to the recorded message on an answering machine which says:

"Hi. You've reached Cindy and Vic. We may or may not be home depending upon who you are. Who are you?"

She says, "Hi, you two, anybody home?"

Cindy quickly picks up the phone and says, "Hello, hello. We're here. Are you still there?"

"Yes, I'm still here."

"Do you have any news about Squeeky?" Cindy says.

"Yes," the veterinarian says, "The tests confirmed my suspicions. Squeeky has hyperthyroidism."

Little Tablets

"Which means exactly what?" I asked Cindy when she told me what the veterinarian had said. "What is hyperthyroidism?" I said, concentrating on pronouncing the word correctly, because the word gave off worrisome vibes. It was the kind of word that if you mispronounced it, worse things might happen.

"OK. This is what she told me. Hyperthyroidism is a condition that's not uncommon among older cats. She said humans can get it, too. What happens with hyperthyroidism is that the thyroid gland starts to excrete excessive amounts of hormones, then the metabolic rate, the rate at which a body consumes calories for fuel and energy gets supercharged, really speeded up. She said some of the key symptoms of hyperthyroidism are increased drinking and urinating, weight loss, and quirky, energized behaviors. Our descriptions of Squeeky's behaviors, along with her age, suggested this condition, and her blood analysis confirmed it."

"So what can be done for her? Did she say how they treat this?" I said, quietly reaching for my stomach, to touch the area that once housed my now long gone appendix.

"She said the most common treatment for this condition is a drug called Tapazole. You usually give it twice a day and it seems to work for most cats with this condition.

"How do you give this Tapazole to a cat?"

"Orally," Cindy said.

"Orally?" I said.

"Yes, orally," Cindy said.

"Is it something you mix in the cat food so the cat can easily eat it?"

"She said they're little tablets that you can break in two."

"What do you do with these little tablets?" I said.

"You open the cat's mouth and you pop them in," Cindy said.

"Is that what the veterinarian said you do?" I said.

"That's what she said," Cindy said.

Popping pills into Squeeky's mouth . . . this was going to be interesting.

Medical Malpractice

The first time we tried to give Squeeky her medicine I held her firmly with both arms, her head up on my shoulder. Cindy readied a half-tablet of Tapazole between her thumb and forefinger. "They're little," the doctor had said. "It'll be easy," she had said. Cheerfully.

"Come on, Squeeky. Let's make this fast," Cindy said, as she pushed the Tapazole toward Squeeky's mouth.

Squeeky looked down at the tablet, sniffed it, quickly concluded that it did not come from anything resembling a tuna or chicken and turned her head away.

"Come on, Squeeky, open up," Cindy said, now holding Squeeky's head with one hand and pushing the Tapazole into her mouth with her other hand. Squeeky refused to open her mouth. You could see Squeeky literally press her little lips together. Her eyes narrowed as determination welled up in her face. Her facial expression said, *"I'll swallow this tablet about as soon as I'll drink from my water bowl."*

But Cindy persisted.

She wedged one finger into Squeeky's mouth, prying it slightly open, just enough to pop the tablet in. After it went in, the struggle stopped. We looked at Squeeky as she looked, somewhat stunned, first at Cindy, then at me, then back at Cindy.

"Did it go down?" I said.

"I think so," Cindy said.

We looked closely at Squeeky, who was now staring at the ceiling, as if there were some interesting artwork up there.

"Did you see her swallow?" I said.

"I'm not sure," Cindy said. "Maybe."

I continued to hold Squeeky in my arms. She didn't squirm as if she wanted to be put down, and she wasn't talking. At all. She acted as if this entire experience was a bit unbelievable.

I put Squeeky down on the kitchen floor and we watched her walk over to the doorway leading to the living room.

"That wasn't too bad," Cindy said. "Maybe she'll get used to taking these things."

Then, just before Squeeky walked into the living room, she turned her head slightly to the left, and spit the tablet on the floor.

I Know, I Know

I tried explaining things to Squeeky as she walked away from us towards the front door. She had had enough of us and wanted to go outside.

"Nobody likes taking medicine," I said to her backside. "I sure don't. But when I have to, I do."

Squeeky walked up to the front door.

"You better do the same. You have to take this stuff, 'cause it might make you feel better," I said, realizing I was verbally reasoning with an animal, and one that was deaf, but her inability to understand what I was saying didn't have anything to do with my need to say it.

Squeeky reached the front door and turned around and went "**WAW0W!**"

"I know," I said. "You're irritated with this whole thing and probably don't feel all that great and just want to go out. I know, I know."

I looked down at Squeeky as she looked up at me, waiting for me to open the door. I reached down and petted her on her head. Then I gave her a couple of quick scratches under the chin. She always liked that.

I picked Squeeky up and pushed her up on my left shoulder so her front legs hung over my shoulder. Squeeky was silent. She never did like being picked up or held for any length of time, and she was probably concerned she was going to get that Tapazole tablet shoved back into her mouth again. I touched my cheek to hers, liking the way her fur felt on my face. As I held her I thought of how I held her those many years ago, when I carried her up and down our street, looking for her home, not realizing at the time that she was already home.

I gave Squeeky a kiss on her cheek and she scrunched up her face. She started to squirm a little, letting me know I had held her long enough. I put her down, opened the door, and as I watched her make her way down the front steps, I wondered how we were going to get Squeeky to take her medicine.

Making Tapazole Tasty

We tried giving Squeeky her medicine again.

Several times.

She resisted every time.

In fact, now when I picked Squeeky up, she'd immediately get a panicked look on her face and quickly flash her eyes around, searching for the fingers that pinched the evil tablet that was about to be jammed down her throat. Not wanting to have anything to do with this situation, Squeeky would push strongly against my chest with her forelegs trying to free herself from my grasp.

Twice Cindy managed to get Squeeky to swallow the pill.

Those were accidents.

It was obvious that struggling with Squeeky every day to give her the medicine was not going to cut it.

She hated those pills, didn't want to have anything to do with them, and began giving us dirty looks.

I'd look down at her, look at her face, and I could clearly read her expression.

"We got along so nicely for fifteen years and now this!

What's the matter with you people?

Why are you doing this?"

Although Squeeky wasn't eating as much as she did in her younger years, when she did eat, she preferred moist cat food to the dry stuff, and always looked up at the kitchen counter for potential snacks, like fresh chicken or turkey. She liked it when you threw a little piece on the floor. It was almost a game to her. Which is how I got the idea of how to get Squeeky to take her medicine.

I took a Tapazole tablet, broke it in two, and wrapped one of the pieces in some sliced smoked turkey. I put it down on the kitchen floor.

Squeeky walked up to it, sniffed it, and in two bites it was gone. She even looked up at me with a renewed attitude of pleasant anticipation, which said: *"Tasty. How about another?"*

Gurgles

As long as Squeeky accepted the chicken or turkey wrapped Tapazole tablets we were doing OK in the thyroid control business. The medicine did its intended job of controlling the amount of hormone produced by Squeeky's thyroid and significantly improved Squeeky's health and behavior.

The medicine didn't affect her talking at all. She continued her yammering ways, from occasional to non-stop, except for those times when she was eating or sleeping or stalking. We took that to be a good sign.

The medicine was powerful ju-ju.

It was no chicken-boned talisman buried upside down on the western slope of a hillside.

Which meant it worked, but any medicine that works may also have some undesirable side effects.

In Squeeky's case, the Tapazole made her throw up.

Not constantly. Not every day. But often enough to make us feel sorry for her and wish she had never developed hyperthyroidism in the first place.

It may not even have been the Tapazole. The veterinarian said that gastro-intestinal upset, resulting in throwing up, was not a common side effect of using Tapazole. But Squeeky's belly said otherwise.

When she was about to throw up, Squeeky always sat down on the floor and faced away from where we were sitting. Like she was being considerate of her company.

"Excuse me a moment, won't you? I'm about to puke"

Then a series of rhythmic gurgles, usually 3 or 4, preceded the upchucking moment. Then came the upchuck.

It wasn't like there was tons of stuff all over the floor.

It was just a little puddle in front of her.

When the gurgles passed, Squeeky usually sat pensively for a moment, as if she was wondering why she just did what she did.

We always told her it was no big deal, and then we wiped it up. That was just the way things were going to be from now on.

Water

One afternoon, Squeeky was lying outside on the walkway to our front steps, and just to keep busy while I kept an eye on our girl, I decided to water the flowers in front of the house. It was a warm day and I was thirsty, so in the middle of watering the flowers, I leaned over and drank from the hose. Squeeky was watching me.

Squeeky had never shown any interest in the garden hose or what came from it before, but this time she got up and came over to me and looked at the steady trickle of water.

I put the hose down on the ground and held up the end where the water came out and Squeeky first sniffed it, then gave the water an exploratory lick. She kept licking and drinking until she was good and full. Then she walked away.

But she didn't go back to her spot on the walkway. She went inside our house directly into the bathroom where she did her two-hop jump onto the bathroom sink and started to howl for somebody to come turn on the faucet.

Another drink?

Just after she had a bunch of water from the garden hose?

I thought that was odd. I knew it was a hot day, but don't you get enough water at some point?

That night, it must have been around 1:00 o'clock in the morning, Squeeky's howling woke me up. She was sitting on the bathroom sink, yammering for somebody to turn on the faucet. I rolled over and pulled the covers up over my head so I wouldn't hear Squeeky's repetitive "yeow . . . yeow . . . yeow."

She had it timed pretty good. She kept going "yeow" without missing a beat for a breath of air.

I thought I should refuse to get up, otherwise I'd be giving in to her, and what if she started doing this every night?

"yeow . . . yeow . . . yeow."

What if she refused to stop until she got her way?

"yeow . . . yeow . . . yeow."

Until somebody got up and turned on the faucet.

"yeow . . . yeow . . . yeow."

Because she wanted water.

"yeow . . . yeow . . . yeow."

But still didn't want to drink from her water bowl.

"yeow . . . yeow . . . yeow.

I pulled the covers tighter over my head.

"yeow . . . yeow . . . yeow."

I pushed the covers into my ears with my thumbs.

"yeow . . . yeow . . . yeow."

"yeow . . . yeow . . . yeow."

Finally, I got out of bed and walked into the bathroom and turned on the faucet.
I realized that I'd be a very weak prisoner of war.

Potato Chips

I thought Squeeky's insatiable desire for water was a one time thing, that maybe it was brought on by the heat of the day or the discovered novelty of drinking from the garden hose. But then why did she want another drink so soon after drinking from the hose outside?

Or maybe it was like eating potato chips, when you're slightly bored and a little hungry. You open a bag just to have two or three chips and pretty soon you're shoving handfuls of potato chips in your mouth and before you know it half the bag is gone.

I thought Squeeky's water drinking was like that.

I thought wrong.

The next day Squeeky woke up in the morning, walked over to her food bowl, nibbled at her food without much enthusiasm, then headed for the bathroom sink.

Whatever she did the rest of day – sleep for a while on her blue shawl on the sofa in the TV room, sit on the window sill in the living room to check out the birds at the feeder hanging from the tree out front, or curl up for an early afternoon catnap on a living room chair – was preceded by a trip to the bathroom sink, followed by her repeated calls for water, for someone to turn on the faucet.

When we let her outside in the late afternoon, she walked down the front steps with a new pattern that would be repeated every time. She went down the steps, and after clearing the last one, she made an immediate right turn and walked over to the garden hose, and started to bellow as loud as she could for someone to come turn on the water.

I didn't get any of this.

Neither did Cindy.

Who had the right idea: call a doctor at the animal hospital for an explanation, which we got, but only after taking Squeeky on another yowling trip to the animal hospital for another examination.

Another Lesson On Cat Physiology

This was the veterinarian's explanation.

"As cats age it's not uncommon for them to experience kidney problems. In veterinary medicine, this condition is referred to as Chronic Renal Failure. The name comes from the names given to an artery and vein that are attached to the kidneys. They're called the renal artery and renal vein.

"Kidney function is extremely important, because in cats, as in humans, kidneys regulate the body's fluids. They control blood pressure, excrete waste material from the bloodstream, affect mineral concentration in body fluids, even get involved in the production of red blood cells.

"If a kidney is severely damaged, as in the case of an accident or serious illness, the only alternative may be a transplant. What's more common, though, is kidney failure due to the slow degenerative process that affects many older cats. Symptoms of weight loss and dehydration typically develop, because the kidneys are no longer able to properly regulate body fluids. Because the cats are dehydrated, they become thirsty and drink more water. But they can only drink enough water to satisfy their fluid needs temporarily. Within hours, they want more water."

I thought that pretty much said it. That described our Squeeky and what was going on with her.

But there was more to know about Chronic Renal Failure.

About how it's a progressive disease, which means it gets worse over time, and time could be months, or it could be years. The thing that varies is the rate at which the kidneys deteriorate, and that would be different for each cat. At present, there was no cure for Chronic Renal Failure, but the condition could be managed with diet and fluids given to the cat. Some cats, according to the veterinarian, could live for several years with fluids given regularly. The frequency of fluid application depended upon the needs of the cat. It could be several times a week, once a week, or every couple of weeks.

"And how are these fluids given? Cindy asked.

"Subcutaneously," the veterinarian replied.

"Subcutaneously," I said to myself, not liking this word any better than hyperthyroidism. I wondered if things would work out if I just let the garden hose run continuously for Squeeky, creating her own personal, never-ending water supply.

The veterinarian continued with her explanation.

"Subcutaneous means under the skin. For cats with kidney problems that are in need of rehydration, a needle is inserted under the skin. The needle is connected to a tube which is connected to a plastic pouch which has the fluids and minerals the cat needs. After the fluid is delivered, the needle is removed, and you're done. It only takes a minute or two."

"What do you mean, 'you're done'?" I said.

"You can do this at home," the veterinarian said.

"Really," I said, politely, not believing that for a minute.

Lewis And Clark

So there we were.

Cindy and I and Squeeky.

Once again standing in front of the kitchen sink, in the same spot where we once tried to give Squeeky a flea bath, then her first Tapazole tablet, we were now going to try to give Squeeky fluids, subcutaneously, via a needle connected to a thin plastic tube which was connected to a pouch that contained the fluid solution that was going to flow down through the tube, through the needle, under Squeeky's skin, replenishing her diminished fluid levels and satisfy her water cravings.

I was going to hold Squeeky still by cradling her in my arms while Cindy inserted the needle into Squeeky's skin in an area just below and in back of her head. Cats seem to have a little extra skin back there. It makes it convenient for mother cats to pick up their kittens when they're in the wrong spot and plop 'em down in the right spot, and for the administration of modern veterinarian practices such as the one we were about to attempt.

After Cindy placed the needle, she would hold it steady with one hand, making sure it didn't slip out, and hold up the fluid-filled pouch with the other hand, creating a gravity-assisted flow of water down to a waiting Squeeky.

I had a pretty good hold of Squeeky, and when Cindy had the pouch and needle ready I said, "Let's do it." As I said this I had a sudden vision. It was of the explorers, Lewis and Clark, in the middle of a great Midwestern plain, tip-toeing up behind a large, wild buffalo, with one of them saying, "Do you want to try and pet it, or shall I?"

We were set.

I had Squeeky, Cindy had the needle and pouch, and as we looked at each other Cindy said, "OK. Are you ready?"

I said, "I'm ready. Are you?"

"Yeah," Cindy said.

"OK, then," I said.

"Here we go," Cindy said.

Cindy inserted the needle.

And Squeeky gave out a good, solid screech like . . . like she'd been stuck with a needle. She never reacted that vociferously when she was at the animal hospital and they gave her a shot. But here, at home, she hollered like she was being tortured. What was it that made it easier to wail and yowl at home? I made a mental note to get a white lab coat. Maybe that was it.

Still holding Squeeky tightly, I said, "Is the needle in? Are the fluids going in?"

I was hoping the fluids would be sucked into her body with a quick and easy "swoosh," so that we'd be quickly done with this adventure. But fluids apparently don't enter a body, whether cat or human, like that. They go in slowly, in a steady stream, allowing the body time to absorb the liquid. It also gives the recipient enough time and energy to generate a series of nicely horrific screams, each one louder than the one before.

Squeeky wailed and wriggled and gave an adrenaline-charged push with her forelegs against my chest and slipped from my grasp. As she jumped out of my arms, the needle popped out from under her skin, slipped out of Cindy's fingers, and squirted the fluid solution all over me. I got a good shot of it in my left eye.

Squeeky started to run away, then stopped, and came back to where Cindy and I were standing. She was curious about the wet stuff all over the kitchen floor. I pointed to it and said, "Try it. You might like it better off the floor."

Squeeky sniffed at the fluids, turned and walked away. She went into the bathroom where she hopped up onto the sink and started chattering.

She was asking for the water to be turned on so she could get a drink.

Because the Los Gatos Dog and Cat Hospital was only a few blocks away, and because Cindy and I realized that Squeeky would never allow us the opportunity of developing an acceptable needle-inserting, fluids-administering technique without either, or both, of us developing a nervous breakdown, we decided to let the vets and techs at the hospital deal with Squeeky. As frequently as Squeeky was going to need fluids, at least once or twice a week, one of us could gladly drive to the hospital, grateful that it was nearby.

What would we have done if the hospital was farther away?

Easy answer.

Move closer.

Fill 'Er Up

Now that we were making frequent trips to the veterinary hospital, Squeeky didn't seem to mind the car trips as much. She didn't holler for as long a time or as loudly, and she always quieted down when we entered the lobby and Marie, the office manager, wearing a sly and infectious grin, would say, "Oh, here's Squeeky. Must be time for another fill-up."

After receiving a pouch-full of fluids, Squeeky's water cravings were satisfied and the frantic edge to her behavior was dulled temporarily.

We'd bring her home from the hospital and if she didn't want anything to eat, she usually went to her blue shawl and slept.

Her relatively calm behavior lasted for a day or two. Then, as her body began to dehydrate, Squeeky got antsy, fidgety. If she was outside she showed little interest in a passing bird. Her attention focused on spots in the front yard where water would collect after a morning's watering. She looked for a possible puddle in the driveway. Sometimes tiny pools would form at the lawn's edge. Failing to find water at those sources, she'd walk up to the curled garden hose and stand by it, hoping that someone would come by and do the magical thing that made the water flow.

At night, she'd often wake us up with her howling as she stood and waited at the sink in the bathroom. Why wouldn't she drink from her water bowl if she was that thirsty? But she didn't. Old habits are hard to break. So either Cindy or I would get up, turn on the faucet, wait until she was finished slurping, then turn off the faucet, pick her up and bring her back to bed.

Squeeky would curl up between us and go to sleep. If she only slept for a short while and soon started pacing throughout the house, winding up back at the bathroom sink, we knew that the next day we had to take her to the hospital for more fluids.

One Other Thing

I was sitting in my leather chair in the TV room with a book in my hands, trying to read, and not able to read. I'd start a paragraph and in the middle of a sentence a herd of wild words and phrases would gallop through my brain. They'd pass, and I'd start the paragraph again, and "baroom, baroom, baroom," they'd come pounding back through again.

I had to stop reading and check 'em out.

It was the old Time Thing again, this time dragging along another Thing for me to think about.

It was another concept that seemed to shadow the Time Thing. It was right there, up close, just a step behind. The more I thought about it, the more I realized it went wherever the Time Thing went. It sat in the Time Thing's back pocket like an old bus ticket.

It was the Youth Thing.

When you're young, you have what seems like an endless amount of time to do all the stuff you want to do, and if you're lucky, the health and energy with which to do it. You think that old age is what happens to other people. Not you.

You have a future of infinite options, and lots of time, so all you have to do is choose which road to take, and if one turns out to be a dead-end, screw it, you'll take another. You are golden. You will be discovered. It's only a matter of time and that's one thing you've got lots of.

What you don't realize when you're young is that someday you will get old. And as you age, you change, mentally and physically.

You learn a few things.

Values and priorities often change.

You gain wisdom. Or maybe get stupider. It can go either way.

Physical changes may be the more difficult of the two to accept, because, as I see it, there's no upside to getting physically older. That's because physical things, whether they're car parts or body parts, eventually wear out and break down. When they break down, you have to repair the broken down parts, or replace them with new ones. If you can.

It was Time Thing's and Youth Thing's fault.

They were like two bandits on horseback, who came and grabbed and stuffed things in their saddlebags and were now galloping, hard, fast, making their getaway. All you see is a cloud of dust. All you hear are the sound of hooves, shrinking towards silence with each passing moment.

"Come back here!" you shout. "What do you have in those bags?"

"What am I missing?" you wonder as you pat your pockets and look around you, not noticing that anything's gone.

Through the dust, you can't even see if they turn around to acknowledge that they heard you. They just keep on riding.

I looked over at Squeeky who was sitting by the back door in a shaft of warm sunlight with her eyes closed. She had some broken down body parts that now required attention: ears that no longer heard, a thyroid on overdrive, kidneys on underdrive, and legs and joints getting a little stiff from arthritis.

I told her, "If the Time Thing and the Youth Thing come through here again, let's kick their ass."

How It Goes

Our Squeeky had gotten old.

Our little girl was a girl no longer. She was now a senior, with some of the maladies that afflict other seniors.

Squeeky, who used to be meticulous in her cleaning habits, regularly licking her backside and belly, washing her cheeks with her moistened paws after eating, now hardly cleaned herself at all and sometimes didn't smell good. Funny. I thought that was true only of old men. At least she didn't smoke cigarettes.

There was no way of knowing her exact age since she didn't come to us with a birth certificate, but we had guessed that she was about one year old when she first walked across our patio. Since she had been with us for about 19 years, that put her age at right around 19 or 20.

I don't know how that translates into human years.

Having had a couple of dogs when I was a kid, I learned that one dog year is roughly equivalent to seven human years. So when a dog is, say, 13 or 14, he's in his 80s or 90s.

But what's the ratio of cat years to human years? 1 to 7 seems a bit high. Because if that ratio was accurate, and Squeeky was 20, that would make her 140 years old! Wow! Is that what eating tuna every day can do for you?

1 to 5 seems a little better. That would have put Squeeky at 100.

None of the numbers seemed possible. Either the 140 or the 100 or the 19. But the regular trips to the animal hospital for fluids and the medicine we gave her daily for her thyroid made the numbers real. Squeeky was old, and her health was fading, and there was nothing we could do about it.

Except continue to love her and care for her and do everything we could for her well-being.

Now, Cindy and I both took a little extra time when petting Squeeky or getting her food or hoisting her up on the bathroom sink for her drink of water.

We often told her how much we loved her. 'Cause once you realize how quickly time can vanish, time becomes more precious, and you start making the most of it, before there's no more time left.

We wondered how much sand was left in the hourglass, knowing that someday it would run empty. Someday. That's the day that always comes sooner than anyone expects.

.

Saturday Night

It was a Saturday night and I was lying on the bed reading, Squeeky lying next to me on my left side. Cindy was watching TV.

As I held the book with my right hand, I had my left arm around Squeeky, and occasionally petted her backside and stroked her stomach. I noticed that her belly felt a little fuller and looked a bit more rounded than it had in some time. Over the last several years Squeeky had lost a few pounds and had gotten noticeably thinner. She still ate something every day, but she had become a finicky eater. Her eyes no longer widened with excitement and anticipation when I opened a new can of cat food. She also didn't eat as much because she was now relatively inactive as compared to her energetic, younger days. She simply didn't burn up as many calories as she used to. Also, Cindy thought the thyroid medication may have affected her appetite. On many days, Squeeky was listless and lay around most of the day. She was not real perky. Consequently, she didn't eat much. You put all these conditions together and you have a cat that's going to lose some weight.

So I was glad to feel Squeeky's belly. If she really had gained a little weight, I thought maybe her overall health was improving.

Then I noticed Squeeky's breathing. With every exhalation, her whiskers twitched and the skin on her snout slightly fluttered.

I watched Squeeky for a while, watched her breathing.

When Cindy came into the bedroom I said, "I think Squeeky's breathing funny."

Cindy came up beside the bed and petted Squeeky and looked at her closely.

Squeeky continued sleeping, but her breathing seemed labored. She didn't wake or stir when Cindy petted her.

"Let's keep a close eye on her," Cindy said. "The hospital's closed tomorrow, but Monday I'll take her in first thing and let one of the docs take a look at her.

On Sunday, Squeeky slept most of the day and had very little to eat. By most measures, it was another typical day. Periodically I'd look at Squeeky while she slept. She seemed to be OK, but her breathing was shallow, short intakes followed by puffy exhalations. Something wasn't right.

Monday Morning At 8:00 AM

As I walked out of our house on Monday morning I said "Good luck with Squeeky," to Cindy. She was going to take Squeeky to the hospital and have her checked out, see what was up with her irregular breathing.

I said "Good Luck" with no more urgency than if I had said "Have a nice day."

Because this day was going to be pretty much like all the other days of the past 19 years. Wasn't it?

Why wouldn't it?

The sun rose as people stirred, and eyes and ears everywhere opened to the possibilities of another day.

As I'd go to work I'd listen to some music or maybe some news or maybe throw in a cassette or CD recording of, say, early Rolling Stones, like their 12 X 5 album, or if I was in a mood I'd put in Neil Young's "Harvest Moon" and listen to the title song for at least the 101st time and try to harmonize along with the background vocals, and when I'd finish playing that song I'd go back to the radio because I rarely listened to a complete album or CD of anybody anymore. I just listened to my favorite songs. Then I'd punch a few music stations trying to find some new music that I cared to listen to, and not hearing anything I liked, again, I'd realize that I was getting older and there seemed to be fewer new songs that I really liked every year because the new stuff was being written by those young enough to call me "grandpa," and they had something going on internally that I didn't have. Working as an outside sales rep I'd make five or six sales calls every day. The usual "blah, blah, blah." And "How about some blah, blah?" Or "We have a new blah blah. Wanna see?" Then I'd have lunch, think about buying a lotto ticket, but only if the jackpot had gotten up there, make the final sales call, then drive home to more music and news and see Cindy and Squeeky, then have dinner and if the lawn didn't need mowing or the patio swept clean of leaves or whatever chores needed to be done, we'd watch some TV, deciding who got to sit next to Squeeky on the sofa as she slept on her blue shawl.

I could have done days like that forever.

Which would have meant that things never change.

Never ever.

But it's not like that, is it?

It's not like Lester's Orchard was still around.

Monday Morning At 10:00 AM

I was at one of my accounts, a health food store, when Cindy called. It was mid-morning, around 10:00. One of the girls at the customer service desk who happened to know me came up to me as I was presenting some new products to the vitamin buyer and said, "There's a call for you on line one. It's your wife."

As I walked over to pick up the phone I wondered what she was going to say, what the doctor had said about Squeeky.

I was hopeful and apprehensive at the same time. I wanted Squeeky's problem to be nothing serious, for it to go away, for it to be somehow treatable. But, then, you never know.

"Hi," I said. "What's the news?" I asked the question trying to put a positive, upbeat spin in my voice as if that might influence what I was about to hear.

"I'm at the hospital," Cindy said, flatly. "It's not good. You need to come. Right away."

I paused for a second or two, to let Cindy's somber tone of voice and the brevity of her comments sink in. Sometimes the less you say is the more you say, and the less you say is enough.

"I'm on my way," I said.

Briefcase

I hung up the phone and felt my anxiety increase.

The news was serious enough that I needed to go to the hospital right away, but why didn't Cindy say what the problem was?

Maybe they didn't know. Maybe the diagnosis was too complex, would take some time to explain, and Cindy didn't want to tie up the hospital's phone line. Maybe there were options to discuss.

After I hung up the phone I felt uncertainty and nervousness swell within me like a balloon.

I hurried from the store to the parking lot. When I got to my car I realized I wasn't carrying my briefcase. Where was it?   I couldn't remember if I had left it somewhere inside the store. Perhaps at a buyer's desk. I wondered where it was. I couldn't even remember if I had brought it into the store in the first place. Maybe I had left it at home. I thought to go back inside and look for it. It wouldn't take me long. Or should I just go? I stood outside my car and I didn't know what to do.

Should I go back inside and look for the briefcase?

Or should I leave and come back later and look for it?

I knew I had to go, but I wanted to know where my briefcase was.

There wasn't anything valuable in it. Just order forms and stuff. Everything in it, including the briefcase itself, was replaceable.

I stood outside my car, my hand on the door handle. At that moment everything seemed to quiet down, all the activity in the parking lot slowed, the noise of car engines and people talking receded to a hushed muffle. It was almost peaceful.

I felt a strange calmness, as I waited for a voice to tell me that I really didn't have to go to the hospital after all. It could have been the voice of one of the sales personnel, running into the parking lot, looking for me, finding me, then shouting, "Wait, you don't have to go!

Or the person might have been holding a cell phone, giving it to me and saying, "It's your wife. She says it's OK now!"

But there was no such voice.

I got in the car and drove to the hospital, not caring if I ever saw the briefcase again.

At The Hospital

When I got to the Los Gatos Dog and Cat Hospital, I was directed to one of the exam rooms, where I found Cindy and Squeeky and Doc Jennifer. Squeeky sat in the middle of an exam table. Doc Jennifer and Cindy were standing. Cindy had her arm around Squeeky.

As I entered the room, everybody looked at me, including Squeeky. I looked at her, at her blue eyes and her beautiful face of chocolate colors and white streaks and brown swirls, and she appeared no differently than she had for the past 19 years. I mean, she looked good. She looked OK. Sitting on the table, she looked like she could have been sitting in the middle of our front yard, waiting for the sun to come up over the roof of our house, so she could lay down and stretch out in the warm sunshine. What was the problem? Why were we here?

Standing there, with Cindy and Squeeky and Doc Jennifer, I sensed the strange calmness that I had noticed earlier in the parking lot. A surreal quality defined the moment. Time stopped momentarily, pausing, holding its breath. I was there and not there at the same time. I became aware of where I was and what I was doing more as an observer rather than a participant. I felt like I was not in my body. When I spoke I came back to my body. I addressed no one in particular, and spoke to the room, when I asked, "What is it?"

Doc Jennifer explained to me, as she had to Cindy, that Squeeky's lungs and stomach cavity were slowly filling with fluids. Which was why her belly had swelled a bit, and why she had difficulty breathing. Doc Jennifer had given Squeeky a diuretic to release some of the water, but that was only a temporary solution to make Squeeky more comfortable. She said you could not continue to give diuretics indefinitely. What was happening to Squeeky was that her kidneys were failing. Her kidneys were no longer able to process and eliminate her body's fluids, so her cavities, her lungs and her stomach, were filling with these fluids.

Doc Jennifer said that Squeeky's condition was irreversible. That she had done well to make it this far, given her hyperthyroidism and her fluid needs for the last several years. But now, Squeeky's quality of life was rapidly deteriorating. We couldn't just take Squeeky home and hope that she would somehow get better. That wasn't going to happen. There was no medicine that could reverse the passage of time or rejuvenate the deteriorating organs within Squeeky's aged body.

Doc Jennifer said it was her best medical opinion that it was time to help Squeeky as we did many years ago, when we decided to give her a home and treat her with care and love for all the years of her life.

We now needed to make another decision, so Squeeky would not suffer any more discomfort or pain that might lie ahead.

If we wanted to, Doc Jennifer said, we could go home and come back a little later. She said she would make sure that Squeeky was comfortable until we returned.

We told her that was what we were going to do.

That we needed to go home.

And then we'd be back.

Why We Went Home

We went home because we needed time, any time, the tiniest bit of time available, to breathe more deeply and clear our minds, to find strength within ourselves to make the most difficult decision either of us had ever had to make.

Being able to return to our small, old house was comforting. It was our home. Cindy's and mine and Squeeky's. Every room, all the nooks and crannies in the front and back yards were filled with lots of images and moments of joy and expressions of love and shared happiness. It was a good old house that the three of us had shared for 19 years.

There was little to discuss. There really was no other viable option. Had there been any alternative choices, Doc Jennifer would have presented them, and we would have taken any one, or all of them, whatever the cost.

We told one another that we knew this day would come eventually. And now it was here. In the past, I sometimes wondered what it would be like. Now I knew. I wasn't ready for it. Deep down inside, I knew I would never be ready for it.

We didn't stay home for very long. Just long enough to find the courage to go back to the hospital and say what needed to be said, and let Doc Jennifer do what needed to be done.

75 Pounds Of Sadness

We drove back to the hospital. I don't remember if we said anything. All I know is that it was a grey January day and I felt as if whatever was happening was not really happening. As I drove I could feel my eyebrows furrow and tighten. It felt like they were knotting with tiny weights forming over my eyes, and my eyes could not support the weight over them, so eventually, my eyebrows would force my eyes to close. A deep sadness grew within me and spread throughout my body. I felt heavier. My arms and legs felt thicker, like I had gained an extra 75 pounds and now I could hardly move. It was the weight of sadness. 75 pounds was about the right measure for this sadness. Other sadnesses could be lighter or heavier. This one was about 75 pounds.

Time To Say Goodbye

We entered the lobby and Cindy went back behind the counter to let Doc Jennifer know we were there. A few minutes later, a door to the lobby opened. It was Cindy. She said, "We're in here."

I entered the room, and again, there stood Cindy and Doc Jennifer. Squeeky sat in the middle of the exam table. She was comfortable. Doc Jennifer had taken good care of her.

It was time. Not for discussion or decision. That was over. It was time to say goodbye.

Cindy, with tears in her eyes, leaned over Squeeky, kissed her on her forehead and said, "I love you Squeeky. You'll always be my little girl."

Cindy hugged her and then stepped back. It was my turn.

I walked up to Squeeky and petted her on her head and along her backside. I looked at her very closely. At the outline of her face, forehead, ears, chin. I wanted them to burn into my memory.

I kissed Squeeky on the side of her face and she scrunched up her eyes because she never did like a big fuss made over her.

I said, "I love you Squeeky. I'll never forget you."

I wanted to say something more. I struggled to find some additional words. But tears came, I couldn't see very well, I couldn't think clearly, and I could barely breathe.

I stepped back and Doc Jennifer said to both of us, "Will you stay?"

Cindy said yes she would. She had the strength to stay which amazed me.

I shook my head and turned and went out the door that opened into the lobby and walked outside into the parking lot. And I cried. Big, heavy sobs, each one a torturous protest, that today, right now, something that had been a part of my life, was now being ripped from me, tearing a hole in my heart, leaving behind an indescribable ache. I cried because I knew the ache was real, it belonged to me, and it could not be fixed.

Someone from the hospital, it could have been one of the doctors or one of the attendants, touched my shoulder as I stood in the parking lot and said, "You should come back inside."

"No," I said. "I can't," not looking at the person

"Yes, you can," she said. "You should. It'll be O.K."

I went back inside.

In the room, there were only Cindy and Squeeky.

Cindy was standing and crying and petting Squeeky, who was lying on her side, now lifeless.

I walked up to the table and Cindy said, "You should pet her. It's your last chance."

And I stroked Squeeky's soft fur one last time.

Then we went home.

Leaves

When we got home, our house was quiet.

It had become a sad, old house. A grainy black and white photograph into which we had walked. It didn't feel right to be there, but where else could we have gone?

We walked into the living room and Cindy sat down on the sofa. I didn't feel like sitting down so I walked into the kitchen. There, on the floor, Squeeky's food bowl sat half full. I realized that the bowl didn't have to be there any more, and the food had to be discarded, but I left it there, for the time being. I walked into our TV room that was in the back of the house and looked at the back door, then down to the lower right window panel that had framed Squeeky's face whenever she wanted to come back in after she had been outside for a while, that she had looked through when she first came to us. I looked over at the sofa. Squeeky's blue shawl was neatly folded, lying over one of the sofa arms. I walked back into the living room and walked over to the front window and looked out onto the street.

I wasn't there, for the final moments, in the exam room. I couldn't stand to be there, so I had to ask Cindy.

"What do they do when they put an animal to sleep?"

"They give them a shot of a barbiturate. It's an anesthetic." she said.

"Is it painful?"

"No. The action of the barbiturate isn't painful. It's a shot like any other shot an animal might get."

"Is it fast?"

"Yes. It's an overdose quantity that's used, and it immediately stops the heart. It happens very fast."

I thought about things happening fast, or at least seeming to, like the way 19 years went by like they were a summer vacation.

I said, "I can't believe she's gone."

"I know," Cindy said. "I can't believe it either."

We had both cried until our eyes ran out of tears, and after the tears were gone, all that was left was a dull, throbbing ache inside.

The sorrow grips your sides and squeezes you, and you think if you listen carefully you might hear the snapping sound of tiny bones cracking, like dry leaves being stepped on.

Ashes

Even as we agonized over losing Squeeky, yet another decision, the final one, was thrust upon us.

What were we to do with Squeeky's remains?

Should we bury her at home? Place her in a pet cemetery? What?

"What do you want to do?" Cindy asked.

It's unfortunate when choices must be made during times of grief. A coherent statement indicating a preference, a direction, a desired action is required, and all you really want to do is lie somewhere quiet and dark and let someone else decide for you. But that doesn't happen. So you breathe deeply and force your brain to form a thought, your mouth to say something intelligible. The best I could do was to say, "I don't know."

Then we discussed the options.

Neither of us was crazy about the pet cemetery idea. I didn't know where the nearest one was located, but wherever it was, as I pictured it, it seemed . . . too impersonal and too far away. Maybe what really bothered me is that a cemetery seemed too final.

Then we thought we could bury her on our property, in the back yard with the big Eucalyptus tree and juniper bushes, through which she had walked straight into our lives. Our house and property had become her home and would be a suitable final resting place. That seemed appropriate.

Then Cindy brought up another topic, one we had discussed off and on the last few years. It was the idea of our possibly moving somewhere else, away from downtown Los Gatos. We wanted to see more trees and countryside, and fewer retail stores and the people they attract. We wanted to hear birds in the morning instead of the mechanical buzz of commute traffic.

That created a problem.

"I hate the idea of our moving and leaving Squeeky here," Cindy said. "It doesn't seem right."

The more I thought about it, it did feel strange. Somehow, should we do that, bury her on our property and then sell the house and move, it seemed like we would be abandoning her. That might sound foolish or silly, I know. But if we moved, it would not be without feeling sad to leave the house and neighborhood we had lived in for almost 30 years. And to think that Squeeky would still be there, without us, was not an acceptable scenario.

We would not bury her.

We chose cremation. As we learned, when a pet is cremated the ashes can be appropriately disposed, or the owners may receive the ashes, which is what we decided to do.

Squeeky's ashes were returned to us. In a white urn. In the shape of a curled-up, sleeping cat.

Memories

In the days that followed, images of Squeeky constantly darted into our minds and conversation. Whether we were at home watching TV, or walking downtown, or anywhere doing anything, whoever had the memory would just start talking, "Remember when . . ." and then recall how it was:

When we first saw her, first heard her, trying to find out to whom she belonged, deciding on her name, letting her into our home,

her adventures with squirrels and birds and lizards,

the sound of her eating,

how it felt to have her sleeping in bed with us, the weight of her tiny body pressed up against a hip,

petting her and feeling the softness of her fur as she stretched out because she liked the gentle movement of a hand caressing her,

saying to Cindy, "There. Up There. See? That's where she is. You were wondering where she was and she's up there on the roof, sleeping in a bunch of leaves."

coming home and seeing her at the back door, looking up at us through the lower right hand corner window pane, starting to talk, because she was glad to see us, and how we opened the door to let her in, because we were always glad to see her.

The Return Of The Time Thing

We felt terrible.

It was a gnawing, gritty sense of sorrow that wouldn't go away.

We had lost our Squeeky.

She had become as much a part of our lives as any family member, and meant as much as anything either of us had ever had.

Squeeky was Cindy's first pet. Her mother had severe asthma and couldn't have cats or dogs in the house. Besides, she liked parakeets.

I simply grew to love Squeeky more than the dogs I had as a child. I now realized I was a cat man.

Others sympathized with our grief and were well-intentioned when they suggested that we get another pet. "Go right away and get another one. Adopt one," they said. "It'll make you feel better."

That might work for some folks. But for us, it wasn't so easy.

It was not like replacing a broken dish or a car that stopped running or a lost family heirloom. This was different.

It took the Return of The Time Thing to help us out a little. The effects of The Time Thing seem to appear when you least expect them. They are quite subtle.

What we found out was that the pain of loss diminishes a tiny bit with each passing day, but it never completely goes away.

That's OK. We don't want it to.

It reminds us of how much we loved Squeeky.

The Lucky Ones

I wondered if all pet owners, when their pets died, experienced what we were going through.

I came to the conclusion that not all did.

Only the lucky ones.

The ones fortunate enough to accept an animal into their lives and lovingly care for it for all of its days.

I think the caring of an animal gives us humans the opportunity to show some of the better aspects of our nature, which is a mishmash of psychological and sociological needs, pulled and pushed by the circumstances of politics and economics and religion, the expectations of family and friends, and all the rest of it.

Pets allow us to daily demonstrate kindness and patience. They respond to goodness. They are our companions regardless of our status or financial position. Their affection for us is independent of fashion or season.

Our relationships with them are less complex than they are with people, easier to understand, free of envy, the need to impress. Our conversations with them are free of nuances and hidden meanings. Time spent with our pets, whether at play or rest, is by turns enriching, soothing, revitalizing. Those are our rewards.

A pet encourages us to behave as we should toward each other, and when you do that for any time at all, it makes you a better human being.

It's good to be needed. To be helpful. To share. To make things better for someone else. Squeeky was our someone else.

We were lucky to have Squeeky come into our lives. Realizing this helped to cope with losing her.

Coming Home

Several weeks later we received the urn that held Squeeky's ashes. Now, she would always be home, with us.

Along with the urn, the folks at the pet cemetery had sent a condolence letter, which offered appropriate sentiments. That was appreciated.

They also sent some information about "The Rainbow Bridge."

It was the first I had ever heard of this "Rainbow Bridge."

I'm not sure about the possible existence of either heaven or hell, but The Rainbow Bridge has some real possibilities.

The Rainbow Bridge

Just this side of heaven is a place called The Rainbow Bridge. When an animal dies that has been especially close to someone here, that pet goes to Rainbow Bridge. There are meadows and hills for all our special friends so they can run and play together. There is plenty of food, water and sunshine, and our friends are warm and comfortable.

All the animals who had been ill or old are restored to health and vigor; those who were hurt or maimed are made whole and strong again, just as we remember them in our dreams of days gone by. The animals are happy and content, except for one small thing; they each miss someone very special to them who had to be left behind. They all run and play together, but the day comes when one suddenly stops and looks into the distance. His bright eyes are intent; his eager body quivers. Suddenly he begins to run from the group, flying over the green grass, his legs carrying him faster and faster.

You have been spotted, and when you and your special friend finally meet, you cling to each other in joyous reunion, never to be parted again. The happy kisses rain upon your face; your hands again caress the beloved head and you look once more into the trusting eyes of your pet, so long gone from your life but never absent from your heart.

Then you cross Rainbow Bridge together . . . . .

Author Unknown

Until Then

See you, Squeeky.

Postscript: A Final Note

No one knows exactly how many homeless cats there are.

"Some feline experts now estimate 70 million feral cats live in the United States."
(National Geographic News, Sep. 7, 2004)

Organizations

Many national and local organizations exist to serve the needs of our animal populations, ranging from providing information on animal care, to creating shelters for abandoned animals. Some, especially the local rescue organizations, are a wonderful resource for pet adoption. If you're not able to personally use the services of any of these organizations, consider making a contribution to support their work. What they do can change an animal's, or a person's, life forever.

- American Humane Association
  (303) 792-9900
  www.americanhumane.org

- American Society for the Prevention of Cruelty to Animals
  (800) 628-0028
  www.aspca.org

- American Veterinary Medical Association
  (847)925-8070
  www.avma.org

- Best Friends Animal Sanctuary
  (435) 644-2001
  www.bestfriends.org

- Consult your phone directory for your local animal welfare and rescue groups.

Special Thanks

To Cindy, who was always there for Squeeky.

To the doctors and staff of Los Gatos Dog and Cat Hospital, Los Gatos, Ca. Your service and support were above the norm, and will never be forgotten. Thank you again.

To Dr. Tom Strolle, a veterinarian at Best Friends Animal Clinic, Grass Valley, Ca. Dr. Strolle not only reviewed the medical information for accuracy, but also demonstrated a talent for copy-editing.

To Karen Harper Barone, an extraordinary artist, who created the original cover art of Squeeky.

To John Leonard of Grass Valley, Ca., who was the first to read this story. He offered constructive criticism, sage advice, support and encouragement, and finally, designed the front and back covers.

Printed in the United States
131778LV00003B/73/A